LOW-FAT RECIPES MASTERY

3 in 1

A Low Fat Cookbook with Over 150 Quick & Easy Recipes

Ward, Wood, Cox

All rights reserved.

Disclaimer

The information contained i is meant to serve as a comprehensive collection of strategies that the author of this eBook has done research about. Summaries, strategies, tips and tricks are only recommendation by the author, and reading this eBook will not guarantee that one's results will exactly mirror the author's results. The author of the eBook has made all reasonable effort to provide current and accurate information for the readers of the eBook. The author and it's associates will not be held liable for any unintentional error or omissions that may be found. The material in the eBook may include information by third parties. Third party materials comprise of opinions expressed by their owners. As such, the author of the eBook does not assume responsibility or liability for any third party material or opinions. Whether because of the progression of the internet, or the unforeseen changes in company policy and editorial submission guidelines, what is stated as fact at the time of this writing may become outdated or inapplicable later.

The eBook is copyright © 2021 with all rights reserved. It is illegal to redistribute, copy, or create derivative work from this eBook whole or in part. No parts of this report may be reproduced or retransmitted in any reproduced or retransmitted in any forms whatsoever without the writing expressed and signed permission from the author

Sommario

A Low Fat Cookbook with Over 50 Quick & Easy Recipes 11
INTRODUCTION 13
JACKET POTATOES WITH HERB QUARK 20
PASTA SALAD 22
PAPRIKA RICE 24
BELL PEPPERS WITH COUSCOUS VEGETABLE FILLING 26
PAPAS ARRUGADAS (SALT AND SHRIVELED POTATOES). 28
PANNA COTTA WITH MILK 30
PANNA COTTA WITH MILK 32
ORIGINAL SPAETZLE DOUGH 34
ORANGE AND MINT YOGURT 36
OVEN TOMATOES 38
BAKED POTATO WITH COUSCOUS FILLING 40
BAKED CHICKEN 42
FRUIT SALAD WITH YOGURT 44
FRUIT SALAD WITH FRESH GINGER 46
NOODLE SOUP FROM VIETNAM 48
PASTA SALAD WITH HERB SAUCE 50
PASTA WITH CHILLI AND ONIONS 52
NIGIRI SUSHI 54
NEAPOLITAN TOMATO SAUCE 56
CLAM SALAD 58
HOUSEWIFE-STYLE MUSSELS 61

MORO CARROT SOUP	63
CARROT SALAD	65
CARROT STEW WITH GINGER	66
CARROT AND TURMERIC SOUP	69
CARROT CURRY SOUP	71
CARROT SPREAD WITH GINGER	72
MINESTRONE	74
MINESTRONE WITH BEANS	77
RICE PUDDING WITH RICE MILK	79
RICE PUDDING FROM THE STEAMER	81
MELON SALAD WITH FETA	83
HORSERADISH SALAD	85
MANGO COCONUT MUESLI	87
MAKI SUSHI	89
CORN SAUCE	91
CREAM OF CORN SOUP WITH POTATOES	93
LOW CARB ONION TART	95
LENTIL SOUP WITH TOFU	97
LENTIL SOUP WITH HERDER CHEESE	99
LIME YOGURT DRESSING	101
LIGHT VEGAN PUMPKIN SOUP	102
LEEK CASSEROLE WITH MINCED MEAT	104
LAMB MEDALLIONS	107
SALMON FILLET ON RISOTTO	109

SALMON WITH FRENCH BEANS	111
SALMON FROM THE STEAMER	113
PUMPKIN SOUP WITH MARJORAM	115
PUMPKIN HUMMUS	117
CREAM OF PUMPKIN SOUP WITH COCONUT MILK	119
CONCLUSION	121
INTRODUCTION	125
PUMPKIN COCONUT SOUP	132
PUMPKIN AND GINGER SOUP	134
CABBAGE SOUP FOR DIET	136
KOHLRABI SPREAD	138
CRISPY PAN BREAD	140
CRUNCHY YOGURT MUESLI	142
CRUNCHY SHAKE FRIES	144
CLEAR CHICKEN BROTH	146
KIWIGELÉE	148
KISIR	150
KIDNEY BEANS WITH AVOCADO	152
CHICKPEA SALAD	154
CHICKPEA SUGO	156
CHICKPEA AND AVOCADO SALAD WITH QUINOA	158
POTATO SOUP WITH PEAS AND DANDELIONS	160
POTATO SOUP WITH BROCCOLI	162
SWEET AND SOUR POTATOES	164

POTATO DUMPLINGS WITH SPINACH 166
POTATO GOULASH 168
POTATO WEDGES IN THE OVEN 170
POTATO WEDGES MADE FROM SWEET POTATOES 172
POTATO WEDGES FROM THE AIR FRYER 174
MASHED POTATOES WITHOUT BUTTER 176
PAN-FRIED POTATOES 178
POTATO AND VEGETABLE PAN WITH EGG 180
POTATO AND PEA PUREE 182
CARAMELIZED FENNEL 184
VEAL STOCK OR VEAL BROTH 186
STEAMED COD WITH RADISHES 188
COD WITH MUSHROOMS 190
YOGURT GRANOLA WITH BANANA 192
YOGURT GARLIC SAUCE 194
YOGHURT HONEY MUSTARD DRESSING 196
ITALIAN BREAD SALAD - PANZANELLA 198
ITALIAN ONION SOUP 200
GINGER JAM WITH ORANGES 202
GINGER-LEMON DIP 204
INDIAN PRAWN CURRY 206
CHICKEN FILLET WITH MUSHROOMS AND PARSLEY 208
ITALIAN STYLE CHICKEN BREAST STRIPS 210
MILLET PORRIDGE WITH GRAPES 212

MILLET COMPOTE WITH APPLE AND CINNAMON	214
HOT GAZPACHO	216
HARE WITH HUNTER SAUCE	218
HAND CHEESE WITH MUSIC	220
GRUEL	222
OAT GROATS WITH BANANAS	224
OATMEAL DRINK	226
CHICKEN BREAST STRIPS WITH PAPRIKA	228
CHICKEN BREAST SALAD	230
CONCLUSION	232
INTRODUCTION	235
ZUCCHINI SALAD	241
ZUCCHINI DRESSING	243
WATERMELON SALAD WITH FETA	244
WHOLE FOOD CASSEROLE WITH POTATOES AND TOMATOES	246
WHOLE GRAIN STICKS	248
VEGETARIAN POINTED CABBAGE STEW	250
VEGETARIAN SOLYANKA	252
VEGAN CHILLI	254
VEGAN TOMATO DIP	256
VEGAN MANGO LASSI	258
VEGAN STOCK POT	260
VEGAN FROZEN YOGURT	262
VEGAN CREAM CHEESE MADE FROM CASHEW NUTS	264

VEGAN MUSHROOM SPREAD 266
VEGAN SPREAD WITH BEETROOT AND HORSERADISH .268
VEGAN OVERNIGHT OATS WITH STRAWBERRIES............270
VEGAN MOUSSAKA 272
VEGAN LENTIL SOUP..275
VEGAN PUMPKIN SOUP 277
VEGAN GUACAMOLE..279
VEGAN BROCCOLI CREAM SOUP WITH WHITE BEANS...281
VANILLA SAUCE WITHOUT SUGAR...283
BAKED FENNEL WITH MOZZARELLA...285
FANTASTICALLY SWEET YEAST DOUGH..................................287
TOMATOSOUP...289
TOMATO SOUP WITHOUT SUGAR 291
TOMATO SOUP WITH RICE 293
TOMATO SOUP WITH PEARL BARLEY 295
TOMATO RAGOUT WITH EGGPLANT 297
TOMATOES FILLED WITH SPINACH...299
TOMATOES WRAPPED IN CUCUMBER 301
COLD TOMATO BOWL...303
TOMATO AND CUCUMBER STICKS 305
THAI SWEET AND SOUR SAUCE 307
SWEET POTATOES WITH COTTAGE CHEESE......................309
SWEET POTATO SALAD WITH SPINACH..................................311
SWEET POTATO CURRY CHIPS..313

SWEET CARROTS 315
SWEET PUMPKIN RAW FOOD 316
SWEET AND SOUR CHINESE CABBAGE SALAD 317
TURBOT WITH SEAWEED AND ORANGE SALAD................. 319
MUSTARD CRUST STEAK... 321
POINTED PEPPERS FILLED WITH TOFU 323
POINTED PEPPERS WITH COUSCOUS................................... 325
POINTED CABBAGE WITH DRESSING.................................... 328
ASPARAGUS WITH SALMON FILLET FROM THE STEAMER
.... 330
ASPARAGUS FROM THE ROMAN POT.. 332
ASPARAGUS FROM THE STEAMER WITH WILD GARLIC
PESTO 334
SIMPLE RAW SALAD DRESSING 336
SELLERY SOUP... 338
CONCLUSION 340

LOW-FAT RECIPES

A Low Fat Cookbook with Over 50 Quick & Easy Recipes

Ellis Cox

All rights reserved.

Disclaimer

The information contained i is meant to serve as a comprehensive collection of strategies that the author of this eBook has done research about. Summaries, strategies, tips and tricks are only recommendation by the author, and reading this eBook will not guarantee that one's results will exactly mirror the author's results. The author of the eBook has made all reasonable effort to provide current and accurate information for the readers of the eBook. The author and it's associates will not be held liable for any unintentional error or omissions that may be found. The material in the eBook may include information by third parties. Third party materials comprise of opinions expressed by their owners. As such, the author of the eBook does not assume responsibility or liability for any third party material or opinions. Whether because of the progression of the internet, or the unforeseen changes in company policy and editorial submission guidelines, what is stated as fact at the time of this writing may become outdated or inapplicable later.

The eBook is copyright © 2021 with all rights reserved. It is illegal to redistribute, copy, or create derivative work from this eBook whole or in part. No parts of this report may be reproduced or retransmitted in any reproduced or retransmitted in any forms whatsoever without the writing expressed and signed permission from the author

INTRODUCTION

A low-fat diet reduces the amount of fat that is ingested through food, sometimes drastically. Depending on how extreme this diet or nutrition concept is implemented, a mere 30 grams of fat may be consumed per day.

With conventional wholefood nutrition according to the interpretation of the German Nutrition Society, the recommended value is more than twice as high (approx. 66 grams or 30 to 35 percent of the daily energy intake). By greatly reducing dietary fat, the pounds should drop and / or not sit back on the hips.

Even if there are no prohibited foods per se with this diet: With liver sausage, cream and French fries you have reached the daily limit for fat faster than you can say "far from full". Therefore, for a low-fat diet, mainly or exclusively foods with a low fat content should end up on the plate - preferably "good" fats such as those in fish and vegetable oils.

WHAT ARE THE BENEFITS OF A LOW-FAT DIET?

Fat provides vital (essential) fatty acids. The body also needs fat to be able to absorb certain vitamins (A, D, E, K) from food. Eliminating fat in your diet altogether would therefore not be a good idea.

In fact, especially in wealthy industrial nations, significantly more fat is consumed every day than is recommended by experts. One problem with this is that fat is particularly rich in energy - one gram of it contains 9.3 calories and thus twice as many as one gram of carbohydrates or protein. An increased intake of fat therefore promotes obesity. In addition, too many saturated fatty acids, such as those in butter, lard or chocolate, are said to increase the risk of cardiovascular diseases and even cancer. Eating low-fat diets could prevent both of these problems.

LOW FAT FOODS: TABLE FOR LEAN ALTERNATIVES

Most people should be aware that it is not healthy to stuff yourself into uncontrolled fat. Obvious sources of fat such as fat rims on meat and sausage or butter lakes in the frying pan are easy to avoid.

It becomes more difficult with hidden fats, such as those found in pastries or cheese. With the latter, the amount of fat is sometimes given as an absolute percentage, sometimes as "% FiTr.", I.e. the fat content in the dry matter that arises when the water is removed from the food .

For a low-fat diet you have to look carefully, because a cream quark with 11.4% fat sounds lower in fat than one with 40% FiTr .. Both products have the same fat content. Lists from nutrition experts (e.g. the DGE) help to integrate a low-fat diet into everyday life as easily as possible and to avoid tripping hazards. For example, here is an instead of a table (high-fat foods with low-fat alternatives):

High fat foods

Low fat alternatives

Butter

Cream cheese, herb quark, mustard, sour cream, tomato paste

French fries, fried potatoes, croquettes, potato pancakes

Jacket potatoes, baked potatoes or baked potatoes

Pork belly, sausage, goose, duck

Veal, venison, turkey, pork cutlet, -lende, chicken, duck breast without skin

Lyoner, mortadella, salami, liver sausage, black pudding, bacon

Cooked / smoked ham without a fat rim, low-fat sausages such as salmon ham, turkey breast, roast meats, aspic sausage

Fat-free alternatives to sausage or cheese or to combine with them

Tomato, cucumber, radish slices, lettuce on bread or even banana slices / thin apple wedges, strawberries

Fish sticks

Steamed, low-fat fish

Tuna, salmon, mackerel, herring

Steamed cod, saithe, haddock

Milk, yoghurt (3.5% fat)

Milk, yoghurt (1.5% fat)

Cream quark (11.4% fat = 40% FiTr.)

Quark (5.1% fat = 20% FiTr.)

Double cream cheese (31.5% fat)

Layered cheese (2.0% fat = 10% FiTr.)

Fat cheese (> 15% fat = 30% FiTr.)

Low-fat cheeses (max. 15% fat = max. 30% FiTr.)

Creme fraiche (40% fat)

Sour cream (10% fat)

Mascarpone (47.5% fat)

Grainy cream cheese (2.9% fat)

Fruit cake with short crust pastry

Fruit cake with yeast or sponge batter

Sponge cake, cream cake, chocolate chip cookies, shortbread, chocolate, bars

Low-fat sweets such as Russian bread, ladyfingers, dried fruits, gummy bears, fruit gums, mini chocolate kisses (attention: sugar!)

Nut nougat cream, chocolate slices

Grainy cream cheese with a little jam

Croissants

Pretzel croissants, whole meal rolls, yeast pastries

Nuts, potato chips

Salt sticks or pretzels

Ice cream

Fruit ice cream

Black olives (35.8% fat)

Green olives (13.3% fat)

LOW-FAT DIET: HOW TO SAVE FAT IN THE HOUSEHOLD

In addition to exchanging ingredients, there are a few other tricks you can use to incorporate a low-fat diet into your everyday life:

Steaming, stewing and grilling are fat-saving cooking methods for a low-fat diet.

Cook in the Römertopf or with special stainless steel pots. Food can also be prepared without fat in coated pans or in the foil.

You can also save fat with a pump sprayer: fill in about half of the oil and water, shake it and spray it on the base of the cookware before frying. If you don't have a pump sprayer, you can grease the cookware with a brush - this also saves fat.

For a low-fat diet in cream sauces or casseroles, replace half of the cream with milk.

Let soups and sauces cool down and then scoop the fat off the surface.

Prepare sauces with a little oil, sour cream or milk.

Roast and vegetable stocks can be tied with pureed vegetables or grated raw potatoes for a low-fat diet.

Put parchment paper or foil on the baking sheet, then there is no need to grease.

Just add a small piece of butter and fresh herbs to vegetable dishes, and the eyes will soon eat too.

Tie cream dishes with gelatin.

LOW FAT DIET: HOW HEALTHY IS IT REALLY?

For a long time, nutrition experts have been convinced that a low-fat diet is the key to a slim figure and health. Butter, cream and red meat, on the other hand, were considered a danger to the heart, blood values and scales. However, more and more studies suggest that fat isn't actually as bad as it gets. In contrast to a reduced-fat nutrition plan, test subjects could, for example, stick to a Mediterranean menu with lots of vegetable oil and fish, were healthier and still did not get fat.

When comparing different studies on fat, American researchers found that there was no connection between the consumption of saturated fat and the risk of coronary heart disease. There was also no clear scientific evidence that low-fat diets prolong life. Only so-called trans fats , which are produced, among other things, during deep-frying and the partial hardening of vegetable fats (in french fries, chips, ready-made baked goods etc.), were classified as dangerous by the scientists.

Those who only or mainly eat low-fat or fat-free foods probably eat more consciously overall, but run the risk of getting too little of the "good fats". There is also a risk of a lack of fat-soluble vitamins, which our body needs fat to absorb.

Low-fat diet: the bottom line

A low-fat diet requires dealing with the foods that one intends to consume. As a result, one is likely to be more conscious of buying, cooking and eating.

For weight loss, however, it is not primarily where the calories come from that counts, but that you take in less of them per day than you use. Even more: (Essential) fats are necessary for general health, since without them the body cannot utilize certain nutrients and cannot carry out certain metabolic processes.

In summary, this means: a low-fat diet can be an effective means of weight control or one to compensate for fat indulgence. It is not advisable to do without dietary fat entirely.

JACKET POTATOES WITH HERB QUARK

Servings:4

INGREDIENTS

- 1   kg Potatoes
- for the herb quark
- 1   TL salt
- 1   Pc Shallot (small)
- 1 Federation chives
- 0.5   Federation   parsley
- 0.5   Federation   chives
- 500 G lowfat quark
- 100 ml   milk
- 1 Tbsp   Creme fraiche Cheese
- 1 prize   pepper

PREPARATION

First wash the potatoes and cook them with the skin in salted water for about 20 minutes.

In the meantime, prepare the herb quark. To do this, peel the shallot and cut it into very fine cubes. Thoroughly wash the fresh chives, a bunch of parsley and dill, shake dry and chop finely.

Mix the fresh herbs with the quark, milk and crème fraîche and season with salt and pepper.

At the end of the cooking time, strain the potatoes, peel them and serve the jacket potatoes with herb quark .

PASTA SALAD

S

Servings:4

INGREDIENTS

- 250 G Penne (durum wheat noodles)
- 200 G Cocktail tomatoes
- 1 Federation basil
- 1 shot olive oil
- 1 shot Balsamic vinegar
- 1 prize   salt

PREPARATION

For the pasta salad, first cook the noodles (penne rigate is best) in a saucepan with salted water for about 10-12 minutes until al dente. The noodles are perfect when they are no longer hard but just firm to the bite. Then drain the pasta through a sieve.

In the meantime, wash the tomatoes and cut them in half. Wash the fresh basil, shake dry and remove the leaves from the stems.

Then put the penne in a bowl, mix with the tomatoes, season with olive oil, balsamic vinegar and salt and finally add the basil leaves.

PAPRIKA RICE

S

Servings:4

INGREDIENTS

- 1 Pc   Bell pepper, yellow
- 2 Pc   Bell pepper, red
- 2 Tbsp   olive oil
- 250 G rice
- 500 ml water
- 1 TL salt
- 0.5 TL   Paprika powder, hot as rose
- 2 Tbsp   Tomato paste
- 2 Tbsp   Parsley, chopped

PREPARATION

Halve the peppers, remove the seeds, wash and cut into very small cubes. Then sauté the pepper pieces in a saucepan with olive oil.

Then add the rice and stir briefly. Pour water on, sprinkle in the paprika powder and salt, bring to the boil and leave to swell for about 10-15 minutes over low heat with the lid closed - until the water is absorbed by the rice.

Finally stir in the chopped parsley and tomato paste into the paprika rice .

BELL PEPPERS WITH COUSCOUS VEGETABLE FILLING

Servings:4

INGREDIENTS

- 8 Pc   Bell pepper, red, green, yellow
- 500 ml   Vegetable broth
- 300 G couscous
- 3 Pc   Shallots, finely chopped
- 0.5 Federation   chives
- 1 prize   salt
- 1 prize   Pepper from the grinder
- 1 prize   sugar
- 1 prize   Curry powder
- 1 TL   Butter, for spreading
- 100 G Cocktail tomatoes

PREPARATION

Wash the peppers, cut off the lid, remove the seeds and then cook in a saucepan with salted water for about 2 minutes and rinse in cold water.

Then bring the vegetable stock to the boil, pour over the couscous and let it soak for a good 10 minutes.

In the meantime, wash the tomatoes and cut them in half. Clean and finely chop the shallots. Wash the chives, shake dry and chop finely.

Then mix the soaked couscous with the shallots, tomatoes and chives and season with salt, pepper, curry powder and sugar.

Fill the peppers with the couscous mixture, coat with butter, put the lid back on, place the peppers in a baking dish (or refractory pan or form) and put them in the preheated oven at around 180 degrees (top-bottom heat) for around 15-20 Cook for minutes.

PAPAS ARRUGADAS (SALT AND SHRIVELED POTATOES)

Servings: 4

INGREDIENTS

- 250 G   sea-salt
- 1 l   water
- 1 kg Potatoes, waxy, small to medium-sized

PREPARATION

Papas Arrugadas is a traditional potato dish from the Canary Islands (Spain). To do this, wash the potatoes well and place them with enough water to just cover them all in the pot.

Add the salt, bring the unpeeled potatoes to the boil, switch back to medium heat and cover the pot with a lid so that the water can evaporate.

Now cook the potatoes gently for about 20 to 25 minutes (depending on the size of the potatoes) until they are soft, but they should not become mushy.

Then pour off the cooking water, wipe the pot dry and put it back on the switched-off oven plate for about 30 minutes. The potatoes evaporate and get a whitish, light salt crust - they also take on the typical wrinkled appearance.

PANNA COTTA WITH MILK

S

Servings:4

INGREDIENTS

- 200 ml   milk
- 600 ml   Buttermilk
- 1 Pc   Vanilla pod
- 2 Tbsp   Sugar, fine
- 5 Bl   Gelatin, white

PREPARATION

First soak the gelatin in a bowl of cold water for 5 minutes. Cut the vanilla pod lengthways with a sharp knife and scrape out the pulp.

Put the milk with the sugar in a saucepan, add the vanilla pulp and the vanilla pod and bring to the boil.

Now bring the vanilla milk to the boil for about 1 minute, then take it off the stove, remove the vanilla pod, squeeze out the gelatine and add leaf by leaf to the hot milk and stir in until it has dissolved.

Then let the milk mixture steep for about 10 minutes, then stir in the buttermilk.

Now rinse 4 dessert glasses with cold water, pour in the milk mixture and refrigerate for at least 5 hours.

Then serve the panna cotta with milk well chilled in glasses or turned upside down on serving plates.

PANNA COTTA WITH MILK

S

Servings:4

INGREDIENTS

- 750 ml   Whole milk
- 1 Pk   vanilla sugar
- 4 Tbsp   sugar
- 1 TL   Agar-agar, heaped
- 1 TL   Vegetable oil, neutral
- 4 Pc   Dessert bowls, á 200 ml

PREPARATION

First put the milk in a saucepan and add the sugar and vanilla sugar. Then stir in the agar and bring the milk to the boil, stirring constantly.

Bring the milk to the boil for about 2 minutes, then reduce the temperature and simmer the milk gently over medium heat for about 10 minutes. Stir it again and again.

In the meantime, brush the dessert bowls lightly with vegetable oil. Pour the milk into the molds and let cool down a little.

Then cover with cling film and let cool in the refrigerator for at least 4 hours.

The panna cotta with milk served in either the bowl or the bowl of dip briefly in hot water and the dessert then pounce on plate.

ORIGINAL SPAETZLE DOUGH

S

Servings:5

INGREDIENTS

- 500 G Flour, white, type 405
- 5 Pc Eggs, size M
- 1.5 TL salt
- 1 prize   Salt, for the cooking water
- 250 ml   Water, lukewarm

PREPARATION

For the original spaetzle dough, put the ingredients such as flour, eggs and salt together in a bowl and stir. Then gradually add the water and beat well with the mixing spoon.

The dough should be able to beat bubbles and be able to be pulled up with the mixing spoon. Adjust the consistency with the water. Then cover the bowl and let it rest briefly, about 10 minutes.

In the meantime, bring the salted water to the boil, then spread the dough thinly in portions on a damp spaetzle board and cut fine strips into the water with a scraper (or knife) and leave to stand.

The finished spaetzle come up very quickly and can be skimmed off.

ORANGE AND MINT YOGURT

S

Servings:4

INGREDIENTS

- 4   between   mint
- 1 Pc   Orange, ripe, organic
- 200 G   Natural yoghurt
- 1 prize   sugar
- 1 prize   salt
- 1 prize   pepper

PREPARATION

First wash the fresh mint, shake it dry and chop it finely.

Wash the ripe orange with hot water, dry with kitchen paper and finely rub the peel. Then cut the pulp into small pieces.

Then mix the yoghurt with the mint, the orange pieces and the orange peel and season with salt, pepper and sugar.

OVEN TOMATOES

S

Servings:4

INGREDIENTS

- 4   Pc Medium sized tomatoes
- 2   TL olive oil
- 2   Tbsp   Parmesan, grated
- 0.5 Federation   parsley
- 8   Bl   basil
- 0.5 TL   Oregano, dried

PREPARATION

Pre heat the oven to 180 degrees celcius.

Cut the tomatoes in half and place them on a baking sheet with the cut side up.

Peel and roughly chop the garlic cloves. Wash and chop the parsley and basil.

Spread the garlic, parmesan and spices on the tomatoes, drizzle everything with oil and cook in the oven for 20 minutes until soft and baked.

BAKED POTATO WITH COUSCOUS FILLING

Servings:4

INGREDIENTS

- 4   Pc Potatoes, large, mostly waxy
- 1 prize   salt
- 1 prize pepper
- 1 Tbsp   olive oil
- 150 G tomatoes
- 1 Pc   cucumber
- 0.5 Federation   Spring onion
- 1 Tbsp   Lemon juice
- 8 Tbsp   Grated Gouda
- 4 Tbsp butter
- 4 Tbsp Quark, for garnish

for the couscous

- 125 G couscous
- 125 ml water
- 1 shot olive oil
- 1 TL salt

PREPARATION

Preheat the oven to approx. 175 ° C top and bottom heat. Wash the potatoes, dry them thoroughly and then, wrapped in aluminum foil, cook in the oven for about 2 hours.

In the meantime, bring the couscous to the boil together with the water (or vegetable stock), salt and a dash of olive oil, remove the saucepan from the hotplate and leave it covered for about 5 minutes.

Then wash the tomatoes, cucumber and spring onion and cut into small pieces. Then mix the vegetables with the couscous and season with lemon juice, olive oil, salt and pepper.

When the potatoes are fully baked, take them out of the oven, open the aluminum foil and cut into the potatoes lengthways. Mash the contents of the potatoes a little with a fork, add grated cheese and butter and allow to melt.

Finally, pour the couscous salad over the potatoes and garnish with a spoonful of quark.

BAKED CHICKEN

s

Servings:52

INGREDIENTS

- 700 G Potatoes
- 2 Pc   Garlic cloves
- 3 Tbsp   olive oil
- 1 prize   salt
- 1 prize   Ground pepper
- 700 G   Chicken fillet
- 150 G Mozzarella

PREPARATION

First preheat the oven to 200 ° C top and bottom heat / 180 ° C circulating air.

Then wash the potatoes, peel them and cut them into pieces about 1 centimeter thick.

Then peel and finely chop the garlic and place in a bowl with the potatoes.

Now mix the potatoes with salt, pepper and olive oil, place in a baking dish greased with butter and bake in the oven for 15 minutes.

In the meantime, wash the chicken fillets and pat dry with a little kitchen paper.

Next, take the baking dish out of the oven, slide the potatoes to the edge of the dish and place the chicken fillets in the center.

In the next step, put the whole thing in the oven again for 25 minutes.

Finally, cut the mozzarella into slices, place on the baked chicken and bake for another 2 minutes.

FRUIT SALAD WITH YOGURT

S

Servings: 4

INGREDIENTS

- 2 Pc   Bananas
- 2 Pc   Apples
- 2 Pc   Pears
- 2 Pc   Oranges
- 300 G Grapes, seedless
- 200 G Blueberries
- 4 Tbsp   Lemon juice
- 500 G Natural yoghurt
- 1 TL   honey
- 1 Pk   vanilla sugar

PREPARATION

First wash the grapes, dry them with kitchen paper and cut them in half. Rinse the blueberries briefly and pat dry. Peel the oranges and cut them into pieces.

Then wash the apples and pears, quarter them, remove the cores and cut the fruit into small pieces.

Next, peel and slice the bananas and place in a bowl with the rest of the fruit. Mix everything together carefully and drizzle with half of the lemon juice.

Mix the remaining lemon juice with the yoghurt, honey and vanilla sugar and pour into four bowls.

Finally, distribute the fruit on top and serve the fruit salad with yogurt immediately.

FRUIT SALAD WITH FRESH GINGER

Servings: 4

INGREDIENTS

- 250 G Grapes, seedless
- 1 Pc Honeydew melon
- 1 Pc lemon
- 1 Tbsp Sugar, brown
- 2 cm Ginger, fresh
- 2 Pc orange

PREPARATION

Peel the honeydew melon, remove the stones and cut the pulp into cubes. Then peel the oranges, remove the white skin and fillet the oranges.

Wash, sort and halve the grapes. Peel the ginger and grate it very finely. Halve the lemon and squeeze out the juice.

Now mix the honeydew melon, oranges and grapes in a bowl with sugar, lemon juice and ginger.

Then let the fruit salad with fresh ginger marinate in the refrigerator for 30 minutes.

NOODLE SOUP FROM VIETNAM

S

Servings:4

INGREDIENTS

- 300 G roast beef
- 3 Tbsp soy sauce
- 2 Pc Garlic cloves
- 1 Federation Asian basil
- 500 G Rice noodles
- 1 Federation Coriander, fresh
- 5 Pc spring onions
- 2 l beef broth
- 4 Pc Lemon wedges
- 6 Tbsp Bean sprouts

PREPARATION

For the noodle soup from Vietnam, prepare the rice noodles according to the instructions on the package. Some are only briefly doused with boiling hot water, others have to be soaked in hot water.

Then divide the pasta on 4 deep soup plates.

Cut the roast beef into fine strips and mix with the soy sauce.

Finely chop the Asian basil and coriander and place on the table with the bean sprouts and the lemon wedges in bowls.

Wash and clean the spring onions, cut into fine rings and also place them in bowls on the table.

Spread the roast beef strips on the rice noodles and pour the boiling beef stock over them.

PASTA SALAD WITH HERB SAUCE

Servings:2

INGREDIENTS

- 150 G Corkscrew pasta
- 1 prize   Salt, for cooking
- 1 Pc   Spring onion, with green
- 40 G Bündner meat, thinly cut.

for the sauce

- 0.5 Pc   clove of garlic
- 3 Tbsp   Chervil, finely chopped
- 1 Tbsp   Dill, finely weighed
- 1 Tbsp   Chive rolls
- 120 G Cream thick milk, 10% fat
- 4 Tbsp   Kefir, low fat
- 1 TL   Molkosan
- 2 prize   pepper

- 2 prize   salt

PREPARATION

First cook the noodles in boiling salted water according to the instructions on the packet until they are al dente.

In the meantime, wash and clean the spring onions, cut the greens into fine rings and finely dice the tuber.

Then cut the Bündner meat into fine strips and fill a bowl with the onions.

Pour the pasta into a sieve, rinse, drain well and add to the ingredients in the bowl.

Now peel off the garlic, mash it with a fork and mix it with the herbs in a second bowl with the thick cream milk. Now stir in the kefir, molkosan, pepper and salt until smooth.

Finally, season the sauce again and fold into the pasta mixture. Let the pasta salad with herbal sauce soak for about 15 minutes.

PASTA WITH CHILLI AND ONIONS

Servings:4

INGREDIENTS

- 2 Pc   Chili peppers
- 500 G Pasta
- 5   l   Salt water
- 2 Pc Paprika, red
- 1 Msp Cayenne pepper
- 250 G Canned tomatoes
- 250 G onion
- 1   Bl   parsley
- 1 prize   salt
- 1 prize   Ground pepper

- 5 Tbsp olive oil

PREPARATION

First cook the pasta in a saucepan with salted water for about 10 minutes until al dente.

Meanwhile, peel the onions and cut into thin rings.

Then wash, dry, halve, core and cut the peppers.

Then fry the peppers together with the onions in a saucepan with oil over medium heat for 4-5 minutes.

Now add the tomatoes along with a little salt, pepper and cayenne pepper and cover and simmer for 20 minutes.

In the meantime, drain the pasta and drain well in a sieve.

Next, wash, dry, halve, core and finely chop the chilli peppers.

Then wash, dry and finely chop the parsley.

Then put the chopped chillies together with the noodles in the pot and mix everything well.

Finally, distribute the noodles with chilli and onions on plates, garnish with the parsley and serve.

NIGIRI SUSHI

s

Servings:4

INGREDIENTS

- 1 Cup Sushi rice
- 1.5 Cup water
- 300 G   Salmon fillet
- 5 Tbsp   Rice vinegar
- 1 Tbsp   sugar
- 0.5 Tbsp salt

PREPARATION

First the classic sushi rice is prepared. To do this, wash the rice through a sieve until the water is no longer cloudy.

Then put the sushi rice together with the water in a saucepan and let it soak for around 10 minutes.

Then bring the pot to the boil, reduce the heat and let the rice cook for about 15-20 minutes with the lid closed, until all the water has been absorbed by the rice. Then remove the rice from the hotplate and let it rest for another 5 minutes.

In the meantime, mix the rice vinegar with the sugar and salt in a small bowl and heat up in the microwave.

Then mix the rice vinegar with the rice well.

Now rinse the salmon with cold water, pat dry and cut into pieces approx. 3 cm long and 1 cm wide.

Finally, thin, finger-length rolls are formed from the rice (preferably with wet hands) and each with a piece of salmon.

NEAPOLITAN TOMATO SAUCE

S

Servings:4

INGREDIENTS

- 1 kg   tomatoes
- 1   between   basil
- 1 Pc   clove of garlic
- 2 Tbsp   olive oil
- 1 prize   salt
- 1 prize   Ground pepper

PREPARATION

First wash, dry and roughly dice the tomatoes.

Next, put the olive oil and the tomatoes in a high saucepan and heat everything over medium heat for 4-5 minutes.

In the meantime, wash, dry and finely chop the basil.

Now peel the garlic and add it to the pot together with the basil.

Then cook the tomatoes covered for 20-30 minutes over high heat, stirring occasionally.

In the next step, rub the mixture through a sieve.

Finally, season the Neapolitan tomato sauce with salt and pepper to taste and serve.

CLAM SALAD

S

Servings:6

INGREDIENTS

- 1 Pc   Onion, medium
- 1   kg Mussels, very fresh
- 2 Pc   Garlic cloves
- 2 Tbsp   olive oil
- 250 ml   White wine, dry
- 2 Pc   Tomatoes, fully ripe
- 1 prize   salt
- 1 prize   Ground pepper

For the avocado cream

- 2 Pc   Avocado, ripe
- 2 Tbsp   Lemon juice

- 1 prize   salt
- 1 prize   Ground pepper
- 1 Pc   clove of garlic
- 1 Tbsp   olive oil

PREPARATION

First cut off the whiskers (if any) from the mussels. Then fill a sink with cold water and rinse and clean the mussels thoroughly - changing the water 1-2 times. The mussels are clean when no more sand settles on the pool floor. Sort out opened mussels!

Then peel the onion and garlic and chop very finely. Blanch the tomatoes in boiling water for 2 minutes, rinse with cold water and peel off the skin. Then cut the tomatoes in half, remove the seeds with a spoon and cut the pulp into small pieces.

For the avocado cream, cut the avocados in half, remove the stone and remove the pulp with a spoon. Peel and roughly chop the garlic.

Then put half of the pulp with the lemon juice, garlic and olive oil in a mixing bowl and puree with a cutting stick.

Finely dice the remaining avocado, fold in, place the avocado kernel in the cream and season the cream with salt and pepper.

Now heat the olive oil in a large saucepan, add onions and garlic and sweat for about 5 minutes over medium heat.

Then put the mussels in the saucepan, pour in the wine and cook covered for about 10 minutes.

Finally, lift the mussels out of the pot with a slotted spoon, throw away the unopened mussels, remove the remaining mussels from the shell, place in a flat dish and drizzle with the cooking stock.

Pour the tomato cubes over the mussels, season everything with salt and pepper and serve the mussel salad with the avocado sauce and fresh white bread.

HOUSEWIFE-STYLE MUSSELS

s

Servings:4

INGREDIENTS

- 1 kg Mussels, fresh
- 1 Pc onion
- 1 Pc Celeriac
- 100 G Mushrooms
- 90 ml White wine
- 1 Federation parsley
- 2 Tbsp butter
- 1 prize salt
- 1 prize Ground pepper

PREPARATION

First clean the mussels under cold running water with a small brush, sort out the opened mussels and remove the mustache.

Now peel the onion and cut it into fine cubes. Clean the mushrooms and also cut them into cubes.

Next, peel the celery, peel the threads with a knife and cut the celery into fine pieces.

Melt the butter in a saucepan and lightly sauté the onion pieces, mushrooms and celery for 4-5 minutes over medium heat.

Then add the mussels, pour in the wine and simmer over medium heat for about 5 minutes until the shells of the mussels open - sort out the unopened mussels.

In the meantime, wash the parsley, shake it dry, chop it finely and add salt and pepper to the saucepan.

MORO CARROT SOUP

S

Servings: 2

INGREDIENTS

- 500 G   Carrots
- l water
- 1 TL   Salt (3 g)

PREPARATION

For the Morosche carrot soup, simmer the cleaned and peeled carrots in the water for at least 2 hours over moderate heat.

Then finely puree the carrots with a magic wand.

Then top up the boiled liquid again to 1 liter with boiled water.

Finally add the salt, stir, done.

CARROT SALAD

s

Servings:2

INGREDIENTS

- 6 Pc   Carrots, great
- 2 Pc   Oranges, great
- 2 Tbsp   Wheat germ oil

PREPARATION

First wash the carrots, remove the stalk and grate finely with a kitchen grater.

Then halve the oranges, squeeze them with a juicer and put the juice together with the carrots in a bowl.

Pour the wheat germ oil over it, mix everything together well and the carrot salad is ready .

CARROT STEW WITH GINGER

Servings:4

INGREDIENTS

- Chicken broth, strong
- 1 Pc Chilli pepper, red
- 45 G Ginger, fresh
- 3 Pc Garlic cloves
- 4 Pc Onions, red
- 500 ml Carrot juice
- 6 Tbsp Soy sauce, salty
- 2 Tbsp Lime juice

for the deposit

- 300 G Skinless chicken breast fillets
- 125 G Flat rice noodles (Asia shop)
- 450 G Carrots, thick

for the garnish

- 2 Tbsp   Basil leaves, finely chopped
- 2 Tbsp   sesame oil

PREPARATION

First bring the chicken broth to a boil in a saucepan, put in the chicken breast fillets, reduce the temperature and cook the meat covered over low heat for about 10-12 minutes. Then take it out of the broth and let it cool down.

Meanwhile soak the flat rice noodles in lukewarm water for 5 minutes.

Then bring plenty of water to the boil in a saucepan and cook the rice noodles in it over medium heat for about 1-2 minutes. Then drain the pasta, rinse immediately with cold water and drain.

Next, peel the carrots and ginger. Cut the carrots lengthways first into thin slices, then into thin strips. Cut the ginger into thin slices. Cut the chilli pepper lengthways, remove the seeds and then cut into fine strips.

Peel the onions and garlic, cut into thin slices, add to the chicken broth with the ginger and chilli, add the carrot juice and soy sauce and let the soup simmer gently for about 15 minutes over medium heat.

Then put in the carrot strips, cook for about 2 minutes and season with the lime juice.

Finally cut the chicken into thin slices and add to the soup with the noodles.

Before serving, sprinkle the carrot stew with ginger with basil, drizzle with sesame oil and serve very hot.

CARROT AND TURMERIC SOUP

S

Servings:4

INGREDIENTS

- 1 Pc   onion
- 1 Pc   clove of garlic
- 300 G Carrots
- 4 Tbsp   olive oil
- 1 TL   Turmeric, powder
- 1 prize   salt
- 500 ml   water

PREPARATION

First peel and finely chop the onion and garlic. Clean the carrots and cut into slices.

Now heat the oil in a saucepan and sauté the onion and garlic pieces briefly. Then add the carrots and turmeric and pour the water on top.

Salt the soup, bring to a boil and simmer for about 15 minutes.

Finally puree the soup finely.

CARROT CURRY SOUP

Servings:4

INGREDIENTS

- 400 G   Carrots
- 1 Pc   onion
- 850 ml   Vegetable broth
- 1 TL   Curry powder (spicy)

PREPARATION

Peel and dice the onion and carrot beforehand.

Then bring the vegetables to the boil with the broth in a saucepan and simmer covered over medium heat for about 15 minutes.

When the vegetables are done, puree the soup with the hand mixer, stir in the curry powder and bring to the boil again briefly.

CARROT SPREAD WITH GINGER

S

Servings:4

INGREDIENTS

- 1 TL curry
- 2 Tbsp   Lemon juice
- 200 G Carrots
- 250 G Quark
- 4 cm Ginger, fresh
- 150 G Natural yoghurt
- 1 prize   salt

PREPARATION

Peel the carrots and ginger, grate them finely in a bowl and drizzle with lemon juice.

Now stir the quark with the yoghurt in a bowl until smooth. Fold in the ginger with the carrots and season the carrot spread with ginger with salt and curry.

MINESTRONE

S

Servings:4

INGREDIENTS

- 150 G White beans
- 1 Pc Bay leaf
- 1 Federation parsley
- 0.5 Federation thyme
- 1 between rosemary
- 200 G Pea pods
- 2 Pc zucchini
- 2 Pc Carrots
- 200 Kn celery
- 1 Pc paprika
- 1 TL salt
- 0.5 TL pepper

- 2 Stg   leek
- 2 Pc   Garlic cloves
- 40 G   Ditalini, or short tubular noodles
- 1 Tbsp   olive oil
- 1 TL   Parmesan, grated

PREPARATION

Soak the white beans in cold water the night before and leave to stand overnight.

For the minestrone, bring a large saucepan with about 1.5 liters of water to the boil. Rinse the soaked white beans, add them to the saucepan and cook gently over low heat for 30 to 35 minutes.

In the meantime, wash the bay leaf, rosemary, parsley and thyme, shake dry, tie together with kitchen twine and add to the beans.

Then peel the zucchini, carrots and celery and cut into cubes. Clean the leek and cut into thin rings. Chop the peeled garlic. Halve the peppers, remove the seeds, wash and also cut into cubes. Cut the washed pea pods into small pieces.

Add the prepared vegetables to the beans in the saucepan, season with salt and pepper and cook for 20 minutes at a medium temperature.

Then remove the tied herbs from the minestrone, add the noodles and cook for another 8 minutes - until the noodles are firm to the bite.

Finally, season the minestrone with salt and pepper, drizzle with olive oil and sprinkle with grated Parmesan.

MINESTRONE WITH BEANS

Servings: 4

INGREDIENTS

- 150 G Beans, dried, mixed (see recipe)
- 100 G Pancetta, Italian pork belly
- 4 Tbsp olive oil
- 1 Stg leek
- 250 G savoy
- 1 Pc Paprika, yellow
- 2 Pc Zucchini, small
- 1 Can Tomatoes, chopped, á 800 g
- 750 ml Vegetable broth, hot
- 1 prize salt
- 1 prize Pepper, black, freshly ground
- 75 G Parmesan, coarse, freshly grated

PREPARATION

Please note: The beans (mixture of kidney beans, black and white beans) are soaked for at least 12 hours.

The day before, put the beans in a bowl, cover with cold water and soak for at least 12 hours - even better overnight.

The next day, drain off the soaking water and cook the beans in fresh water without salt over low heat for about 1 1/4 hours. Then pour into a sieve and drain.

During this time, clean and wash the leeks and savoy cabbage. Cut the leek into rings and the savoy cabbage into strips. Clean, wash and dice the peppers. Clean, wash and slice the zucchini.

Then dice the pancetta. Heat the olive oil in a large saucepan and fry the cubes of bacon in it for about 3-4 minutes until crispy, then drain on kitchen paper.

Now fry the prepared vegetables in the bacon fat for 3-4 minutes. Add the canned tomatoes, pour in the broth and cover with all ingredients and simmer over medium heat for about 15 minutes.

Finally add the cooked beans to the vegetables, stir in and let them get hot for 5 minutes. The minestrone with beans with salt and pepper and pour into soup plates. Sprinkle with the coarsely grated parmesan and serve immediately.

RICE PUDDING WITH RICE MILK

Servings:2

INGREDIENTS

- 250 G rice pudding
- 1.2 Rice milk
- 1 prize   cinnamon
- 1 prize   cardamom
- 3 Tbsp   Sugar, white
- 1 Pc   Vanilla pod
- 2 Tbsp   Cinnamon sugar

PREPARATION

First put the rice milk in a saucepan and add the rice pudding. Add the cinnamon, cardamom and sugar to the milk as well.

Next, cut open the vanilla pod and scrape out the pulp. Add the pulp and pod to the rice milk, heat everything and bring to the boil for 1 minute.

After boiling, reduce the temperature and simmer the rice pudding with rice milk over low heat for about 25-30 minutes.

Finally, fish out the vanilla pod and fill the rice pudding into portion bowls. Sprinkle with the cinnamon sugar and enjoy.

RICE PUDDING FROM THE STEAMER

Servings:4

INGREDIENTS

- milk
- 400 G   Rice pudding, short grain rice
- 1 TL   Vanilla sugar
- 4 Tbsp   sugar

for the garnish

- 1 prize   Cinnamon powder
- 1 prize   sugar

PREPARATION

To rice pudding in the steamer cook fill the rice, sugar and vanilla sugar in a bet with no holes for the steam oven and these mix well.

Now add the milk and stir well again.

Then fill the steamer and set a temperature of 100 degrees.

Let the rice pudding cook for around 35 to 40 minutes while in use.

Serve with cinnamon and sugar.

MELON SALAD WITH FETA

Servings:4

INGREDIENTS

- 1 Pc   Watermelon, medium-sized (seedless or seedless)
- 100 G Feta cheese, creamy
- 0.5 Federation   mint
- 0.5 Federation   basil
- 1 Pc   lime
- 2 Tbsp   Maple syrup
- 1 prize   salt
- 1 prize   Pepper, black, freshly ground
- 2 Tbsp   olive oil

PREPARATION

First cut the watermelon in half and cut into thick slices. Remove any stones that may still be present, remove the pulp from the skin with a knife and cut into bite-sized cubes.

Then wash the mint and basil, shake dry, pluck the leaves and chop finely.

Next, cut the lime in half and squeeze out. Mix the juice with the maple syrup, oil, salt and pepper.

Put the melon pieces in a bowl, mix in the dressing and herbs. Roughly crumble the feta and add to the salad.

The melon salad with feta mix again and put for 15 minutes in the refrigerator. Serve immediately afterwards.

HORSERADISH SALAD

Servings:4

INGREDIENTS

- 250 G horseradish
- 1 Pc   Apple
- 1 shot   Lemon juice

for the dressing

- 5 Tbsp   Sour cream
- 1 prize   salt
- 1 prize sugar

PREPARATION

For this simple horseradish salad, first peel the horseradish and grate it finely in a bowl.

Also peel and grate the apple and drizzle a little lemon juice.

Then mix the apple and the cream with the horseradish, finally season with salt and sugar.

MANGO COCONUT MUESLI

Servings: 4

INGREDIENTS

- 70 G Desiccated coconut
- 100 G Prunes
- 130 G oatmeal
- 1 Pc mango
- 200 G Curdled milk
- 130 ml milk
- 4 Tbsp orange juice
- 4 Tbsp Honey, liquid

PREPARATION

First roast the desiccated coconut in a pan until golden brown, stirring constantly.

Cut the plums into small cubes and mix with the oat flakes and desiccated coconut.

Peel the mango, cut the pulp into wedges from the stone and dice.

Put the curd in a bowl or shaker and mix with the milk, orange juice and honey.

Portion half of the oatmeal mixture into bowls, distribute the mango pieces on top, pour over the curd and serve sprinkled with the remaining oatmeal mixture.

MAKI SUSHI

Servings:4

INGREDIENTS

- 1 Cup rice
- 2 Cup water
- 4 Pc Nori sheets
- 2 Pc Carrots
- 1 Pc avocado

PREPARATION

Wash out the rice until only clear water runs through it. Then boil in double the amount of water. Let the rice cool while stirring.

Place a nori sheet on the bamboo mat and spread a thin layer of rice on top. Leave a narrow strip free.

Peel the carrot and avocado and cut into fine strips. Place a strip in the middle of the rice and roll it up tightly.

Cut the roll into about 5 equal pieces. Repeat the process with the remaining ingredients and refrigerate until ready to serve.

CORN SAUCE

Servings: 4

INGREDIENTS

- 300 G Corn, canned
- 250 ml   Vegetable broth
- 150 ml   Whipped cream
- 1 Pc   onion
- 1 Pc   clove of garlic
- 50 G   butter
- 2 Tbsp   Lemon juice
- 1 Federation parsley
- 1 prize   salt
- 1 prize   Ground pepper
- 1 shot Oil, for the pot

PREPARATION

First peel the onion and the garlic, chop them finely and sauté gently in a saucepan with oil for 3-4 minutes over medium heat.

Then add 2/3 of the corn kernels together with the vegetable stock and simmer for 10 minutes.

Then add the cream, salt, pepper and lemon juice to the saucepan, mix everything well and simmer for another 15 minutes.

In the meantime, wash, dry and finely chop the parsley.

Then let the sauce cool down for 5 minutes and purée finely with a hand blender.

Finally mix the remaining corn kernels into the corn sauce and garnish with the parsley.

CREAM OF CORN SOUP WITH POTATOES

Servings: 4

INGREDIENTS

- 2 Can Corn, á 425 g
- 2 Pc Vegetable onions
- 300 G Potatoes, floury cooking
- 4 Tbsp Rapeseed oil
- 1.2 milk
- 1 Pc Bay leaf
- 1 TL salt
- 0.5 TL Chilli flakes
- 1 prize Pepper, black, freshly ground
- 3 Tbsp Lime juice

PREPARATION

First peel and finely dice the onion. Peel, wash and roughly chop the potatoes. Then drain and drain the corn and set aside 2 tablespoons of corn kernels.

Then heat half of the oil in a saucepan, fry half of the onion cubes and the potato cubes for about 5 minutes while stirring.

Now add the remaining corn, put in the bay leaf and pour in the milk. Let everything simmer over medium heat and uncovered for about 10 minutes.

Heat the remaining oil in a pan and fry the remaining onion cubes for about 5 minutes until golden brown. Sprinkle with some chili powder and set aside.

Then take the soup pot off the stove, remove the bay leaf and puree the soup with a cutting stick. Season savory with salt, pepper and lime juice.

Arrange the hot corn cream soup with potatoes in warmed soup plates , sprinkle with the remaining corn and the chilli onions and serve immediately.

LOW CARB ONION TART

Servings:2

INGREDIENTS

- 4 Pc   Filo pastry sheets, from the cooling shelf
- 400 G Onions
- 60   G Bacon, mixed, thinly sliced
- 200 G   cottage cheese
- 60   G Sour cream or crème fraîche
- 1 Pc   Egg, size L
- 2 Tbsp   Parsley, chopped
- 0.5 TL   salt
- 1 prize   Pepper, black, ground
- 1 Tbsp   Vegetable oil, for the pan

PREPARATION

First preheat the oven to 165 ° C top / bottom heat.

Then line a tart pan with the filo pastry and set aside.

Next, peel the onions and cut them into very fine cubes. First cut the bacon slices into strips and then into very fine cubes.

Now put the oil in a large pan and heat it up. Add the diced bacon and onion, fry for about 5-6 minutes over medium heat, then remove from heat and let cool.

In the meantime, mix the cottage cheese, sour cream and egg in a bowl. Season with salt and pepper and fold in the chopped parsley.

Finally fold the bacon and onions into the sour cream mixture, mix everything well and pour into the prepared dish.

Bake the low carb onion cake on the middle rack in the preheated oven for about 40-45 minutes until golden yellow. Then take it out of the oven, let it cool down slightly and serve

LENTIL SOUP WITH TOFU

Servings: 2

INGREDIENTS

- 2 Pc Cocktail tomatoes
- 0.5 Pc onion
- 1 Pc clove of garlic
- 1 Tbsp butter
- 1.5 TL Grated ginger
- 450 ml Vegetable broth
- 120 G Lentils, red
- 1.5 TL Curry paste, red
- 200 G tofu
- 1.5 Tbsp Coconut milk
- 1 prize pepper
- 1 prize salt

- 1 prize   Curry powder
- 1 prize   thyme
- 1 prize   Caraway seed

PREPARATION

Peel and chop the onion and garlic. Heat the butter in a saucepan and sauté the onion and garlic pieces in it.

Wash the tomatoes, quarter them, remove the seeds and cut the pulp into pieces. Then stir in the ginger and tomatoes into the onion garlic mixture and cook briefly.

Then pour the vegetable stock on top and add the red lentils. Season the soup with pepper, salt, curry, red curry paste, a pinch of caraway seeds and thyme. Now let the lentil soup boil gently for about 15 minutes.

Cut the tofu into pieces of equal size as desired.

Finally, add the coconut milk to the soup and add the tofu.

LENTIL SOUP WITH HERDER CHEESE

Servings:4

INGREDIENTS

- 100 G lenses
- 650 ml   Vegetable broth
- 2 TL Curry powder
- 2 Stg Celery
- 1 prize   salt
- 1 prize   Ground pepper
- 150 G Shepherd cheese, or cottage cheese
- 1 Tbsp   oil

PREPARATION

First put the lentils together with the vegetable stock and the curry powder in a saucepan, bring to the boil briefly and simmer for around 10 minutes over a medium heat.

In the meantime, wash and dry the celery, remove the celery greens and save. Cut the celery into thin slices or bite-sized cubes, add to the saucepan, add to the lentils and cook for 5-10 minutes.

Then remove the saucepan from the hotplate, chop up the shepherd's cheese, add to the soup, season with salt and pepper and stir well.

Finally, garnish the lentil soup with the celery greens and serve.

LIME YOGURT DRESSING

Servings:1

INGREDIENTS

- 150   Gyogurt
- 1 prize   salt
- 1 prize   pepper
- 2 Tbsp   Herbs, mixed
- 1 Tbsp   Lime juice

PREPARATION

Wash the herbs well, dry them and finely chop them. Then mix the herbs, lime juice, yogurt, salt and pepper in a screw-top jar. Store tightly closed in the refrigerator.

LIGHT VEGAN PUMPKIN SOUP

Servings:4

INGREDIENTS

- 1 Pc   Hokkaido pumpkin
- 500 ml   water
- 1 Can Coconut milk, reduced fat
- 1 Pc   clove of garlic
- 1 Pc   Ginger, about the size of a thumb
- 1 Tbsp   Lemon juice, from bottle
- 0.5 Federation   parsley
- 0.5 TL   turmeric
- 1 TL Ceylon cinnamon
- 1 prize   salt and pepper
- 1 Spr olive oil

PREPARATION

First cut the pumpkin in half, remove the seeds and cut into cubes about 2 centimeters in size.

Then peel and finely chop the garlic, as well as the ginger. Put both in a large saucepan and fry briefly on medium heat with a little oil - not too hot - so that the flavors can develop properly. Then add the pumpkin pieces and fry for a little while.

Now add the cinnamon and turmeric, stir the contents of the pot well and then add the water.

Now let the soup cook on a higher level for about 25-30 minutes. Once the pumpkin is tender, either the hand blender or the potato masher can do its job until the soup becomes creamy. Depending on the consistency, water can possibly be added.

Finally, finely chop parsley, add and let simmer briefly. Now add the coconut milk and lemon juice. Then stir and season with salt and pepper. The light vegan pumpkin soup is ready .

LEEK CASSEROLE WITH MINCED MEAT

Servings: 4

INGREDIENTS

- 800 G Potatoes, waxy
- 300 G leek
- 3 Tbsp olive oil
- 1 Pc onion
- 1 Pc clove of garlic
- 250 G Ground beef
- 1 Tbsp Thyme leaves, fresh
- 200 ml Meat soup
- 1 prize salt
- 1 prize Pepper, black, freshly ground

- 1 Tbsp   butter
- 1 prize   Salt, for the minced meat
- 1 prize Black pepper for the minced meat

PREPARATION

First prepare the vegetables. To do this, clean the leek, wash it thoroughly and then cut it diagonally into thin slices.

Peel and wash the potatoes, also cut into thin slices and place in a bowl with cold water. Peel and finely chop the onion and garlic.

Then heat the oil in a pan and fry the minced meat for about 6 minutes while stirring. Add the onion and garlic cubes and fry for another 5 minutes.

Now put the leek slices in the pan, mix with the mince and cook for another 5 minutes. Season the mince mixture with salt and pepper and stir in the thyme.

Preheat the oven to 180 ° C (fan oven 160 ° C) and grease a casserole dish with butter.

Take the potato slices out of the water, pat dry and then layer them alternately with the leek mixture in the form. Season each layer with salt and pepper and finish with a layer of potato slices.

Next, pour the broth over the leek casserole with minced meat , spread the flakes of butter over it and cover with a sheet of baking paper.

Slide the mold onto the middle rail in the preheated oven and bake for 30 minutes. Then remove the baking paper and bake for another 30 minutes. Take the finished casserole out of the oven and serve in the form.

LAMB MEDALLIONS

Servings: 4

INGREDIENTS

- 2 Pc   Garlic cloves
- 800 G Saddle of lamb fillet
- 0.5 TL   Rosemary needles
- 1 prize   salt
- 1 prize   Paprika powder, noble sweet
- 2 Tbsp   olive oil
- 1 prize   Pepper from the grinder

for the garlic white bread

- 8 Schb   White bread (as desired)
- 2 Pc   Garlic cloves
- 2 Tbsp   Olive oil, for the pan

PREPARATION

First peel the garlic cloves and press them through a garlic press. Then cut the meat, freed from skin and tendons, into approx. 8 slices, each 2 cm thick. Then flatten the meat slightly and rub it with salt, pepper, paprika powder and the garlic.

For the garlic white bread, peel the remaining garlic cloves and press them through a garlic press. Then heat olive oil in a pan, sauté the garlic and then fry the bread slices in the garlic oil until golden brown on both sides - keep them warm on a plate or in the oven.

Now heat the remaining olive oil in the pan, fry the lamb medallions vigorously (about 3-4 minutes per side, turning only once) and sprinkle with rosemary.

SALMON FILLET ON RISOTTO

S

Servings:4

INGREDIENTS

- 2 Tbsp   Vegetable oil
- 1 Pc   Lemon, organic
- 450 G Cherry tomatoes
- 800 G Salmon fillet, skinless
- 1 prize   salt
- 1 prize   pepper
- for the risotto
- 2 Pc   Onions, small
- 150 G Risotto rice
- 500 ml   Vegetable broth
- 100 ml   White wine, dry
- 1 Pc   Zucchini, medium size

- 120 G Olives, black, without a core
- 3 Tbsp   Vegetable oil
- 1 prize   pepper
- 1 prize   salt

PREPARATION

For the risotto, first peel and dice the onions. Heat two tablespoons of oil in a saucepan, sauté the onion cubes, then add the rice and sauté with it.

Gradually pour in the broth and the wine, stirring frequently. As soon as the rice becomes dry, always add a little liquid and cook for a total of 30-35 minutes.

In the meantime, wash and clean the zucchini, peel if necessary, dice and sauté in a pan with a tablespoon of hot oil. Then put aside.

Now wash the lemon vigorously, dry it with kitchen paper and cut four thin slices. Just wash and dry the cherry tomatoes.

For the salmon fillet on risotto, cut the salmon into 4 strips, then season with salt and pepper.

Now heat the oil in a pan, cover each of the salmon strips with a lemon wedge and fry in the hot oil for about 5 minutes, turning once, add the tomatoes and fry.

Finally, add the zucchini mixture to the finished risotto, season with salt and pepper. Serve together with the salmon strips and tomatoes.

SALMON WITH FRENCH BEANS

Servings: 4

INGREDIENTS

- 600 G French beans
- 4 Pc Salmon fillet, 200 grams each
- 2 prize   salt
- 1 prize   Pepper, freshly ground

PREPARATION

At the beginning, water the Römertopf, i.e. soak it in water for at least 10 minutes, this will fill the clay pores and steam will be produced during cooking.

Clean the green beans, wash them in cold water and drain well. Then place in the Römertopf and add a little salt.

Now put the pot in the cold oven and pre-cook it for 30 minutes at 180 degrees.

In the meantime, rinse the salmon with cold water, pat dry with kitchen paper and season with salt and pepper.

After 30 minutes, place the salmon on the green beans, close the lid again and steam for 10 minutes.

Then remove the lid and bake the salmon with green beans for another 10 minutes.

SALMON FROM THE STEAMER

Servings: 4

INGREDIENTS

- 4 Pc Salmon fillets, wild salmon
- 1 shot Lemon juice
- 1 kg broccoli
- 8 Pc Potatoes, waxy, medium-sized
- 50 G Flaked almonds
- 1 TL Parsley, chopped
- 1 Tbsp   Butter or oil
- 1 prize salt

for the sauce

- 200 ml   Whipped cream
- 2 TL butter

- 2 TL   Flour
- 150 ml   Vegetable broth
- 1 prize   salt
- 1 prize   pepper
- 1 TL   Chives, cut into thin rings

PREPARATION

For salmon from the steamer, first fill the steamer with water or broth according to its instructions for use and grease the insert with a little butter or oil.

Peel and wash the potatoes and quarter them lengthways.

Wash and clean the broccoli and cut into florets.

Salt the salmon fillets and drizzle with lemon juice.

Now set the steamer to 90 degrees and first put the potatoes in the steamer. After 20 minutes add broccoli and salmon and cook for 10 minutes.

Make a roux for the sauce. To do this, melt the butter, dust the flour over it and sweat while stirring constantly.

Then stir in the vegetable stock in small portions, stirring constantly, and bring to the boil. At the end add the cream and season with salt, pepper and chives.

In the meantime, roast the almonds without fat in a coated pan - turning them over and over again.

Finally, arrange all the ingredients on plates, serve the broccoli with flaked almonds and the potatoes sprinkled with chopped parsley.

PUMPKIN SOUP WITH MARJORAM

Servings: 4

INGREDIENTS

- 1 kg Pumpkin (e.g. butternut, nutmeg pumpkin)
- 100 ml Sour cream
- 40 G Butter for the pot
- 1 Tbsp Lemon juice
- 600 ml Vegetable broth
- 1 Federation marjoram
- 1 TL salt
- 1 prize pepper
- 1 Msp saffron
- 1 shot Pumpkin seed oil

PREPARATION

For this fine pumpkin cream soup, quarter the pumpkin, peel it, remove the seeds and cut the pulp into cubes.

Then melt the butter in the saucepan and braise the pumpkin cubes in it - cook for about 5 minutes on a low heat.

Now pour the lemon juice and vegetable stock into the pot and simmer gently for about 15-20 minutes until the pumpkin pieces are soft.

In the meantime, wash the marjoram, shake it dry, pluck the leaves and chop finely. Clean the pumpkin seeds well, dry them with a kitchen towel and fry them lightly in a pan (without oil).

Then puree the soup with a hand blender, add salt and pepper to taste, stir in a little saffron and fold in the ham strips again. In addition, you can refine the soup with a little sour cream.

Put the finished pumpkin soup into plates, sprinkle with the pumpkin seeds, spread the marjoram leaves over the top and garnish with a few dashes of pumpkin seed oil.

PUMPKIN HUMMUS

S

Servings:4

INGREDIENTS

- 500 G   Hokkaido pumpkin
- 1 Pc   clove of garlic
- 1 prize   salt
- 1 prize   pepper
- 1 prize   cumin
- 3 Tbsp   Tahini
- 100 G Sun-dried tomatoes

PREPARATION

Wash and divide the pumpkin, remove the seeds and cut into small pieces. Put the pumpkin cut into pieces on a baking sheet lined with baking paper.

Preheat the oven to 220 degrees and bake the pumpkin on the middle rack for 20 minutes until it is soft.

Peel the garlic and roughly chop it together with the sun-dried tomatoes.

Now put the baked pumpkin, garlic, salt, pepper, cumin, tahini and the chopped tomatoes in the food processor and process into a paste. Alternatively, a hand blender can be used for pureeing.

The Kürbishummus still well be drawn in a plastic box in the refrigerator an hour is consumed until it.

CREAM OF PUMPKIN SOUP WITH COCONUT MILK

Servings:6

INGREDIENTS

- 1   Pc Hokkaido pumpkin (500 g)
- 100 ml   Orange juice, freshly squeezed
- 400 ml vegetable stock
- 300 ml   Coconut milk
- 1 TL Chilli flakes
- 1 TL Lime juice
- 1 TL Curry powder
- 1 prize   salt
- 1 TL   Pepper, black, freshly ground

for the garnish

- 1 TL Chilli flakes
- 0.5 Federation   coriander

PREPARATION

Wash the pumpkin, cut in half and remove the seeds and fibers. Then cut the pumpkin flesh into small cubes and place in a saucepan.

Add the orange juice, the chilli flakes, the curry powder, salt and pepper, fill up with the vegetable stock and bring to the boil.

Bring everything to the boil for 1 minute, then cover and simmer on reduced heat for about 20-25 minutes.

In the meantime, wash the coriander, shake it dry and finely chop the leaves.

Now finely puree the contents of the pot with a cutting stick while adding the coconut milk and lime juice.

The pumpkin soup with coconut milk boil again for 1 minute, then pour into a warm plate.

Garnish with a few chilli flakes and coriander leaves and serve immediately.

CONCLUSION

If you want to lose a few pounds, the low-carb and low-fat diet will eventually reach your limits. Although the weight can be reduced with the diets, the success is usually only short-lived because the diets are too one-sided. So if you want to lose weight and avoid a classic yo-yo effect, you should rather check your energy balance and recalculate your daily calorie requirement.

The ideal is to adhere to a gentle variant of the low-fat diet with 60 to 80 grams of fat per day for life. It helps to maintain the weight and protects against diabetes and high blood lipids with all their health risks.

The low-fat diet is comparably easy to implement because you only have to forego fatty foods or severely limit their proportion of the daily amount of food. With the low-carb diet, on the other hand, much more precise planning and more stamina are necessary. Anything that really fills you up is usually high in carbohydrates and should be avoided. Under certain circumstances, this can lead to food cravings and thus to failure of the diet. It is essential that you eat properly. Many statutory health insurance companies therefore offer prevention courses or pay you for individual nutritional advice. Such advice is extremely important, especially if you decide on a weight-loss diet in which you want to permanently change your entire diet. Whether your private health insurance pays for such measures depends on the tariff you have taken out. In the meantime, however, individual nutritional advice has been taken over by many private providers.

LOW-FAT RECIPES IN 30 MINUTES

A Low Fat Cookbook with Over 50 Quick & Easy Recipes

Jennifer Wood

All rights reserved.

Disclaimer

The information contained i is meant to serve as a comprehensive collection of strategies that the author of this eBook has done research about. Summaries, strategies, tips and tricks are only recommendation by the author, and reading this eBook will not guarantee that one's results will exactly mirror the author's results. The author of the eBook has made all reasonable effort to provide current and accurate information for the readers of the eBook. The author and it's associates will not be held liable for any unintentional error or omissions that may be found. The material in the eBook may include information by third parties. Third party materials comprise of opinions expressed by their owners. As such, the author of the eBook does not assume responsibility or liability for any third party material or opinions. Whether because of the progression of the internet, or the unforeseen changes in company policy and editorial submission guidelines, what is stated as fact at the time of this writing may become outdated or inapplicable later.

The eBook is copyright © 2021 with all rights reserved. It is illegal to redistribute, copy, or create derivative work from this eBook whole or in part. No parts of this report may be reproduced or retransmitted in any reproduced or retransmitted in any forms whatsoever without the writing expressed and signed permission from the author

INTRODUCTION

A low-fat diet reduces the amount of fat that is ingested through food, sometimes drastically. Depending on how extreme this diet or nutrition concept is implemented, a mere 30 grams of fat may be consumed per day.

With conventional wholefood nutrition according to the interpretation of the German Nutrition Society, the recommended value is more than twice as high (approx. 66 grams or 30 to 35 percent of the daily energy intake). By greatly reducing dietary fat, the pounds should drop and / or not sit back on the hips.

Even if there are no prohibited foods per se with this diet: With liver sausage, cream and French fries you have reached the daily limit for fat faster than you can say "far from full". Therefore, for a low-fat diet, mainly or exclusively foods with a low fat content should end up on the plate - preferably "good" fats such as those in fish and vegetable oils.

WHAT ARE THE BENEFITS OF A LOW-FAT DIET?

Fat provides vital (essential) fatty acids. The body also needs fat to be able to absorb certain vitamins (A, D, E, K) from food. Eliminating fat in your diet altogether would therefore not be a good idea.

In fact, especially in wealthy industrial nations, significantly more fat is consumed every day than is recommended by experts. One problem with this is that fat is particularly rich in energy - one gram of it contains 9.3 calories and thus twice as many as one gram of carbohydrates or protein. An increased intake of fat therefore promotes obesity. In addition, too many saturated fatty acids, such as those in butter, lard or chocolate, are said to increase the risk of cardiovascular diseases and even cancer. Eating low-fat diets could prevent both of these problems.

LOW FAT FOODS: TABLE FOR LEAN ALTERNATIVES

Most people should be aware that it is not healthy to stuff yourself into uncontrolled fat. Obvious sources of fat such as fat rims on meat and sausage or butter lakes in the frying pan are easy to avoid.

It becomes more difficult with hidden fats, such as those found in pastries or cheese. With the latter, the amount of fat is sometimes given as an absolute percentage, sometimes as "% FiTr.", I.e. the fat content in the dry matter that arises when the water is removed from the food.

For a low-fat diet you have to look carefully, because a cream quark with 11.4% fat sounds lower in fat than one with 40% FiTr Both products have the same fat content. Lists from nutrition experts (e.g. the DGE) help to integrate a low-fat diet into everyday life as easily as possible and to avoid tripping hazards. For example, here is an instead of a table (high-fat foods with low-fat alternatives):

High fat foods

Low fat alternatives

Butter

Cream cheese, herb quark, mustard, sour cream, tomato paste

French fries, fried potatoes, croquettes, potato pancakes

Jacket potatoes, baked potatoes or baked potatoes

Pork belly, sausage, goose, duck

Veal, venison, turkey, pork cutlet, -lende, chicken, duck breast without skin

Lyoner, mortadella, salami, liver sausage, black pudding, bacon

Cooked / smoked ham without a fat rim, low-fat sausages such as salmon ham, turkey breast, roast meats, aspic sausage

Fat-free alternatives to sausage or cheese or to combine with them

Tomato, cucumber, radish slices, lettuce on bread or even banana slices / thin apple wedges, strawberries

Fish sticks

Steamed, low-fat fish

Tuna, salmon, mackerel, herring

Steamed cod, saithe, haddock

Milk, yoghurt (3.5% fat)

Milk, yoghurt (1.5% fat)

Cream quark (11.4% fat = 40% FiTr.)

Quark (5.1% fat = 20% FiTr.)

Double cream cheese (31.5% fat)

Layered cheese (2.0% fat = 10% FiTr.)

Fat cheese (> 15% fat = 30% FiTr.)

Low-fat cheeses (max. 15% fat = max. 30% FiTr.)

Creme fraiche (40% fat)

Sour cream (10% fat)

Mascarpone (47.5% fat)

Grainy cream cheese (2.9% fat)

Fruit cake with short crust pastry

Fruit cake with yeast or sponge batter

Sponge cake, cream cake, chocolate chip cookies, shortbread, chocolate, bars

Low-fat sweets such as Russian bread, ladyfingers, dried fruits, gummy bears, fruit gums, mini chocolate kisses (attention: sugar!)

Nut nougat cream, chocolate slices

Grainy cream cheese with a little jam

Croissants

Pretzel croissants, whole meal rolls, yeast pastries

Nuts, potato chips

Salt sticks or pretzels

Ice cream

Fruit ice cream

Black olives (35.8% fat)

Green olives (13.3% fat)

LOW-FAT DIET: HOW TO SAVE FAT IN THE HOUSEHOLD

In addition to exchanging ingredients, there are a few other tricks you can use to incorporate a low-fat diet into your everyday life:

Steaming, stewing and grilling are fat-saving cooking methods for a low-fat diet.

Cook in the Römertopf or with special stainless steel pots. Food can also be prepared without fat in coated pans or in the foil.

You can also save fat with a pump sprayer: fill in about half of the oil and water, shake it and spray it on the base of the cookware before frying. If you don't have a pump sprayer, you can grease the cookware with a brush - this also saves fat.

For a low-fat diet in cream sauces or casseroles, replace half of the cream with milk.

Let soups and sauces cool down and then scoop the fat off the surface.

Prepare sauces with a little oil, sour cream or milk.

Roast and vegetable stocks can be tied with pureed vegetables or grated raw potatoes for a low-fat diet.

Put parchment paper or foil on the baking sheet, then there is no need to grease.

Just add a small piece of butter and fresh herbs to vegetable dishes, and the eyes will soon eat too.

Tie cream dishes with gelatin.

LOW FAT DIET: HOW HEALTHY IS IT REALLY?

For a long time, nutrition experts have been convinced that a low-fat diet is the key to a slim figure and health. Butter, cream and red meat, on the other hand, were considered a danger to the heart, blood values and scales. However, more and more studies suggest that fat isn't actually as bad as it gets. In contrast to a reduced-fat nutrition plan, test subjects could, for example, stick to a Mediterranean menu with lots of vegetable oil and fish, were healthier and still did not get fat.

When comparing different studies on fat, American researchers found that there was no connection between the consumption of saturated fat and the risk of coronary heart disease. There was also no clear scientific evidence that low-fat diets prolong life. Only so-called trans fats , which are produced, among other things, during deep-frying and the partial hardening of vegetable fats (in French fries, chips, ready-made baked goods etc.), were classified as dangerous by the scientists.

Those who only or mainly eat low-fat or fat-free foods probably eat more consciously overall, but run the risk of getting too little of the "good fats". There is also a risk of a lack of fat-soluble vitamins, which our body needs fat to absorb.

Low-fat diet: the bottom line

A low-fat diet requires dealing with the foods that one intends to consume. As a result, one is likely to be more conscious of buying, cooking and eating.

For weight loss, however, it is not primarily where the calories come from that counts, but that you take in less of them per day than you use. Even more: (Essential) fats are necessary for general health, since without them the body cannot utilize certain nutrients and cannot carry out certain metabolic processes.

In summary, this means: a low-fat diet can be an effective means of weight control or one to compensate for fat indulgence. It is not advisable to do without dietary fat entirely.

PUMPKIN COCONUT SOUP

Servings:2

INGREDIENTS

- 700 G Pumpkin, Hokkaido
- 1 Stg Lemongrass
- 1 Pc   ginger
- 2 TL   olive oil
- 400 ml   Vegetable broth
- 400 ml   Coconut milk, unsweetened
- 1 TL   salt
- 1 TL   Pepper White
- 2 Tbsp   Pumpkin seeds
- 1 Tbsp   sesame

PREPARATION

First cut the pumpkin in half with a sharp knife, cut out the pulp and cut into small pieces.

Then cut the lemongrass into very fine rings and finely grate the ginger.

Now heat the olive oil in a saucepan and sauté the pumpkin, ginger and lemongrass in it.

Then pour in the vegetable stock and coconut milk, bring to the boil briefly and simmer over medium heat for about 30 minutes until the pumpkin is soft.

In the meantime, carefully toast the pumpkin seeds and sesame seeds in a non-oiled pan.

As soon as the pumpkin is soft, puree the soup, season with salt and pepper and sprinkle with the pumpkin seeds and sesame seeds

PUMPKIN AND GINGER SOUP

Servings:4

INGREDIENTS

- 600 G   Hokkaido pumpkin
- Vegetable broth
- 1 Msp Chili powder, hot
- 1 TL curry
- 3 cm ginger
- 1 shot Lemon juice

PREPARATION

Peel the pumpkin, remove the seeds with a spoon and cut the pulp into small pieces. Also peel and chop the ginger.

Cook both in a saucepan with the vegetable stock over a medium flame for 20 minutes until soft.

Then puree the pumpkin and ginger soup with the hand blender and season well with lemon juice, chilli and curry.

CABBAGE SOUP FOR DIET

Servings:6

INGREDIENTS

- 1   kpf White cabbage (approx. 1 kg)
- 5 Pc   Vegetable onions, medium-sized
- 2 Can Tomato pieces (850 ml each)
- 2 Pc   Yellow / green peppers
- 1 kg   Carrots
- 2 Stg leek
- 200 G Celery bulb
- 6 Tbsp   Parsley, chopped
- 2 Pc   Soup cubes
- 1 TL   pepper
- 1 prize   Chilli powder
- 5 water

PREPARATION

For this cabbage soup for diet, first cut the white cabbage into quarters. Remove bad spots and the firm stalk, wash, then cut into large pieces. Peel and dice the onions.

Now remove the stem from the peppers, then cut in half, remove the seeds, wash the halves and cut into strips. Peel the carrots, if necessary, otherwise wash and cut into strips.

Next, clean the leek, cut away the roots and the long leaves, wash thoroughly, cut into 2 halves lengthways, then cut into wider half rings. Peel, wash and dice the celery.

Then bring the white cabbage with 2 soup cubes to the boil in a large saucepan with water, then add the chopped vegetables. After about 10 minutes, pour in the canned tomatoes and cook for another 15 minutes.

Finally, season the soup with pepper and chilli, then sprinkle with the chopped parsley.

KOHLRABI SPREAD

Servings: 2

INGREDIENTS

- 2 Tbsp   Sour cream
- 1 Tbsp   Nuts, chopped
- 0.5 Federation   parsley
- 100 G Kohlrabi
- 100 G cream cheese
- 1 prize   salt
- 1 prize   pepper

PREPARATION

Peel the kohlrabi and grate it into fine grates. Wash the parsley, shake dry and chop into fine pieces.

Now mix the kohlrabi with the parsley, nuts, cream cheese and sour cream in a bowl.

Finally, season the kohlrabi spread well with salt and pepper.

CRISPY PAN BREAD

Servings: 8

INGREDIENTS

- 300 ml   Water, lukewarm
- 4 Tbsp olive oil
- 1 TL   salt
- 500 G wheat flour
- 1 Pk   Dry yeast
- 1 TL   sugar
- 8 Tbsp   Tahini, sesame paste
- 2 Tbsp   Sesame, light

PREPARATION

For the dough, first whisk the lukewarm water with the salt and oil.

Mix the flour, sugar and dry yeast in a bowl.

Then pour the liquid into the dry ingredients and knead everything with the dough hook of a hand mixer to form a smooth dough.

Cover the dough with a kitchen towel and let rise in a warm place for about 1 hour.

Then sprinkle a little flour on a work surface, knead the dough again after resting on it, divide it into 8 equal pieces and shape into balls.

Now gently heat the sesame paste in the microwave (or in a water bath) and stir so that the oil does not settle.

Roll out the pieces of dough into thin flatbreads (about the size of a pan) and spread the sesame paste on both sides and sprinkle with sesame seeds.

Now heat a pan at medium temperature without adding any fat and bake the cakes one after the other on both sides for about 8-10 minutes.

The Crispy pan bread let cool on a wire rack and enjoy the best fresh.

CRUNCHY YOGURT MUESLI

Servings:2

INGREDIENTS

- 100   Ghearty oat flakes
- 50   G Sunflower seeds
- 50 G   Raisins
- 1 prize   salt
- 2   Tbsp   Maple syrup
- 500   G Soy yogurt
- 1 Pk   vanilla sugar
- 50   G   sliced almonds

PREPARATION

For the crispy yoghurt muesli, heat a pan without fat, add the oat flakes, almonds and sunflower seeds and roast until golden brown.

Now add the raisins and salt and stir well. Then drizzle in the maple syrup, mix everything and let it caramelize over medium heat.

Then spread the mixture on a prepared baking sheet lined with baking paper and let cool for 5 minutes.

In the meantime, put the soy yoghurt in a bowl and sweeten with the vanilla sugar.

Then alternately fill the yoghurt and the granola in layers in two tall glasses and enjoy.

CRUNCHY SHAKE FRIES

Servings: 3

INGREDIENTS

- 1 kg   Potatoes, organic
- 2 Tbsp   Sunflower oil
- 2 TL Paprika powder, smoked
- 2 TL salt

PREPARATION

First preheat the oven to 250 ° C (top and bottom heat), wash the potatoes thoroughly, halve them without peeling and cut into narrow sticks.

Then put the potato sticks together with sunflower oil, salt and paprika powder in a light bowl and shake thoroughly until the spices are evenly distributed.

Now line a tray with baking paper, distribute the french fries evenly on it and bake until crispy golden brown for about 25 minutes.

Finally, take the crispy French fries out of the oven and serve as a side dish or with fresh dips (such as ketchup , aioli , garlic dip , etc.).

CLEAR CHICKEN BROTH

Servings:12

INGREDIENTS

- 1   Pc Soup chicken
- 400 G   Roots, carrots, celery, parsley root
- 2.5 water
- 1 Tbsp   salt

PREPARATION

Clean the kitchen-ready chicken inside and out with cold water, as well as the heart and stomach.

Then put the chicken with the innards in a saucepan with cold salted water and slowly cook until soft on a low level, skimming over and over with a scoop.

In the meantime, wash, peel and cut the roots.

After an hour of cooking, add the prepared vegetables to the chicken and simmer for another hour.

When the meat is tender, drain the clear chicken stock through a fine sieve.

KIWIGELÉE

Servings:4

INGREDIENTS

- 4 Pc   Kiwi fruit
- 0.5   Grape juice
- 0.25 TL   vanilla sugar
- 1   TL Agar Agar
- 1 shot Lemon juice

PREPARATION

First peel the kiwifruit, cut into small pieces and then puree with a dash of lemon juice.

Then put the grape juice with the vanilla sugar and the kiwi mixture in a small saucepan, stir and heat carefully.

Then stir the agar agar with 2 tablespoons of grape juice until smooth and stir into the kiwi mixture. Stir over medium heat for about 2 minutes without the liquid starting to boil.

Finally, pour the kiwi jelly from the pot into the dessert bowls and allow to cool.

KISIR

Servings:4

INGREDIENTS

- 200 G   Bulgur, fine, Köftelik
- 150 ml   Water, boiling
- 1 Pc   Medium onion
- 1 shot Vegetable oil, for the pan
- 1 Tbsp   Tomato paste
- 1 Tbsp   Paprika pulp, Acı Biber Salcası
- 1 Msp Ground cumin
- 1 Tbsp   Chilli flakes, aci pul beaver
- 1 shot Pomegranate Syrup, Nar Eksisi
- 0.5 Federation   mint
- 0.5 Federation   Parsley smooth
- 1 Pc   Spring onion

- 1 shot olive oil
- 1 prize   salt
- 1 prize   Pepper from the grinder
- 1 shot Lemon juice

PREPARATION

Put the bulgur in a bowl, pour the boiling water over it, stir briefly and let it soak for around 15 minutes.

In the meantime, peel the onion and sauté in a pan with oil.

Then add the paprika pulp, tomato paste, ground cumin, chilli flakes (= Aci Pul Biber) and the pomegranate syrup (= Nar Eksisi) to the pan with the onions and stir well. Then remove the pan from the hotplate and let it cool down.

Wash the mint and parsley, shake dry and chop finely. Halve the spring onions lengthways and cut into fine rings.

Then mix the bulgur with the onion mixture and stir in the herbs and finely chopped spring onions.

Finally stir in the olive oil into the kisir and season the bulgur salad with salt, pepper and lemon juice.

KIDNEY BEANS WITH AVOCADO

Servings: 4

INGREDIENTS

- 2 Pc   Onions, great
- 2 Can Kidney beans (about 250g)
- 2 Pc   Avocados, ripe (about 180g)
- 1 Pc   lemon
- 2 Tbsp   Rapeseed oil
- 100 ml   Vegetable broth, instant
- 2 prize   salt
- 2 prize   pepper
- 2 TL Horseradish, grated (glass)
- 1carton   cress

PREPARATION

First peel the onions and cut into fine cubes.

Pour the kidney beans into a kitchen sieve, rinse with cold water and drain well.

Halve the avocados lengthways, remove the core, peel the halves and then dice. Then squeeze the lemon and drizzle it over the cubes.

Now heat the oil in a non-stick pan with a high rim and sauté the onion cubes until golden. Deglaze with the vegetable stock and add the beans and avocados. Let everything simmer for about 4 minutes, stirring constantly.

Finally, season the kidney bean vegetables with avocado with salt, pepper and horseradish, sprinkle with the cress and serve.

CHICKPEA SALAD

Servings: 4

- **INGREDIENTS**
- 250 G Chickpeas, dried
- 3 Pc clove of garlic
- 1 Pc onion
- 1 prize   Pepper, freshly ground

for the dressing

- 50 ml vinegar
- 80 ml olive oil
- 0.5 TL   salt

PREPARATION

Soak the chickpeas overnight (at least 12 hours) with three times the amount of water.

Then strain the chickpeas, pour fresh salted water over them and cook for approx. 90 minutes until they are soft. Then drain well in a sieve.

In the meantime, peel and finely chop the onion and garlic and mix with the chickpeas in a bowl.

Mix a dressing from vinegar, oil, salt and pepper and marinate the chickpea salad with it.

CHICKPEA SUGO

Servings: 4

INGREDIENTS

- 1 Pc   Onion, great
- 2 Pc   clove of garlic
- 4 Tbsp   olive oil
- 100 G Tomato paste
- 100 ml   red wine
- 250 G Chickpeas, cooked
- 750 ml   sieved tomatos
- 1 TL   salt
- 1 prize   pepper
- 1 prize   Paprika powder, noble sweet
- 1 TL   Oregano, grated
- 1 TL   Thyme, grated

PREPARATION

First put olive oil in a saucepan, heat it, peel the onion, cut in half and cut into thin slices, then add, as well as peel the garlic, press into the saucepan with a garlic press, sweat for about 10 minutes over medium heat.

Then fold in red wine and tomato paste, add chickpeas and tomato sauce; Season with pepper, salt, nutmeg and paprika powder.

Finally, let the chickpea sauce simmer gently for another 45 minutes, then sprinkle with oregano and thyme towards the end.

CHICKPEA AND AVOCADO SALAD WITH QUINOA

Servings:2

INGREDIENTS

- 200 G Quinoa
- 200 G Chickpeas (in a jar or can)
- 1 Pc onion
- 4 Pc tomatoes
- 200 G Sheep cheese
- 1 Pc Avocado (as ripe as possible)
- 100 G Lettuce

for the vinaigrette

- 1 Tbsp vinegar
- 1 TL mustard

- 1 TL   honey
- 1 prize   salt
- 1 prize   Pepper (freshly ground)
- 3 Tbsp   olive oil

PREPARATION

First rinse the quinoa with hot water and then put it in a saucepan with plenty of boiling water. Let the quinoa simmer for 20 minutes and let it swell for another 5 minutes after the cooking time.

Then mix the quinoa with the cooked or roasted chickpeas.

Now peel, wash and cut the onion into strips. Then wash and quarter the tomatoes. Dice the sheep cheese.

Peel and halve the avocado, remove the core and then cut into wedges. Wash the lettuce and pluck it into bite-sized pieces. Finally mix all the ingredients with the quinoa and chickpeas.

Now mix a vinaigrette made from olive oil, vinegar, mustard, honey, salt and freshly ground pepper and distribute evenly over the salad.

POTATO SOUP WITH PEAS AND DANDELIONS

Servings:4

INGREDIENTS

- 700 G Potatoes, mainly waxy
- 1 Stg leek
- 2 Tbsp   Olive oil, for the pot
- 200 G Peas, frozen
- 800 ml   water
- 2 TL Vegetable broth, powder
- 1 Federation Dandelion leaves, a good handful
- 0.5 Pc Organic lemon
- 100 ml   Oat cream
- 1 prize   salt

- 1 prize   Chilli flakes

PREPARATION

First wash, peel and dice the potatoes. Then clean the leek, cut it lengthways, wash it thoroughly and then cut it crosswise into fine strips.

Then heat the oil in a large stock pot. Sauté the potatoes and leek while stirring. Add the peas and sauté briefly.

Now add hot water and vegetable stock and bring the whole thing to a boil. Cover and simmer the soup over low heat for about 10 minutes, until the potatoes are tender.

In the meantime, rinse the dandelion leaves, shake dry and chop very finely. Then rub the peel of one lemon half.

Stir the oat cream with the dandelion into the soup and season with salt, chilli flakes and the grated lemon zest.

POTATO SOUP WITH BROCCOLI

Servings: 4

INGREDIENTS

- 1 kg Potatoes, floury cooking
- 500 G broccoli
- 1 Pc onion
- water
- 2.5 TL   Vegetable broth, powder
- 1 shot oil

PREPARATION

First wash, peel and dice the potatoes. Then wash the broccoli as well and cut into florets with your hands and a knife. Peel the broccoli stalk and also cut into cubes. Then peel and finely chop the onion.

Then put the potatoes, broccoli and onion in a saucepan and sauté in a little oil over medium heat. Deglaze with water, add vegetable stock and simmer for about 20 minutes.

Then puree the soup finely and serve. The potato soup with broccoli is ready .

SWEET AND SOUR POTATOES

Servings:4

INGREDIENTS

- 500 G   Potatoes, waxy
- 1 TL salt
- 250 G zucchini
- 1 Pc   onion
- 2 Pc   Garlic cloves
- 150 G Spinach leaves
- 200 G Pineapple pieces (can)
- 200 ml   Pineapple juice
- 1 Tbsp   Oil, neutral
- 50 ml Vegetable broth
- 2 Tbsp   Soy sauce, light
- 2 Tbsp   Apple Cider Vinegar

- 1 Tbsp   honey

PREPARATION

First wash the potatoes, put them in a saucepan with salted water, bring to the boil and cook for about 25 minutes until they are cooked. Then strain the potatoes, peel them and cut them into approx. 2 cm cubes.

Wash the zucchini, cut off both ends and also cut the zucchini into cubes.

Sort, wash and drain the spinach. Drain the pineapple pieces in a colander while collecting the juice.

Peel and finely chop the onion and garlic.

Heat the oil in the wok, fry the onion and garlic pieces in it until translucent, then add the potatoes, zucchini and spinach and fry for 2 minutes. Now deglaze the whole thing with pineapple juice, add the pineapple pieces and vegetable stock.

Finally refine the vegetables with soy sauce, apple cider vinegar and honey, add salt and bring to the boil again.

POTATO DUMPLINGS WITH SPINACH

Servings: 4

INGREDIENTS

- 500 G   Potatoes, floury cooking
- 200 G Spinach leaves
- 4 Tbsp   potato flour
- 1 TL   Salt, for cooking
- 1 prize   Nutmeg, freshly grated
- 1 Msp pepper
- 1 prize   salt
- 2 Pc   protein
- 3 Tbsp   Water to mix

PREPARATION

For the potato dumplings with spinach, brush the potatoes thoroughly, then with the skin in a saucepan, just covered with salted water and cook for 30 minutes - until they are soft.

Drain the potatoes, peel them and press them through a potato press while they are still warm. Then mix the potatoes with salt, pepper and nutmeg.

Now clean the spinach, put the vegetables in a bowl with water, pluck the leaves from the stems, then rinse the leaves 2-3 times. Then briefly blanch the spinach in boiling water, squeeze out and cut very finely.

Now mix the spinach together with 3 tablespoons of potato flour and the egg white into the potato mixture.

Then shape the potato dough into dumplings and let rest for about 10 minutes.

Next, put on a saucepan with 1 liter of salted water. Mix the remaining 2 tablespoons of potato flour with a little water, pour into the saucepan and bring to the boil.

Now put the dumplings in the no longer boiling water and let it simmer over a moderate heat for about 15 minutes.

POTATO GOULASH

Servings: 4

INGREDIENTS

- 150 G Celery bulb
- 800 G Potatoes, mainly waxy
- 2 Pc Carrots
- 2 TL Paprika powder, noble sweet
- 500 ml Vegetable broth, hot
- 4 Tbsp Tomato paste
- 1 prize salt
- 1 Tbsp Crème fraîche, or sour cream
- 3 Pc Onions, finely chopped
- 1 TL Clarified butter
- 1 prize Pepper from the grinder
- 1 prize sugar

PREPARATION

For this vegetarian potato goulash, first peel the potatoes, wash them and cut them into approx. 1 cm cubes. Peel and dice the carrots in the same way, but a little smaller. Clean, peel and cut the celery into sticks.

Fry the onions in the clarified butter in a saucepan, then add the diced potatoes and carrots as well as the celery and fry briefly.

Pour the vegetable stock on top, sprinkle with paprika powder and stir in the tomato paste. Put the lid on and cook covered for about 10 minutes until soft.

Finally, season the potato goulash with salt, pepper, sugar and crème fraîche and serve.

POTATO WEDGES IN THE OVEN

Servings: 4

INGREDIENTS

- 850 G Potatoes, waxy
- 4 Tbsp   olive oil
- 2 TL Paprika powder, mild
- 1 TL salt

PREPARATION

First preheat the oven to 200 ° C (convection) or 220 ° C (top and bottom heat) and cover a baking sheet with baking paper.

Peel and wash the potatoes, cut into quarters and then place in a bowl.

Now distribute the olive oil, salt and paprika powder over the potato path and mix thoroughly with your hands.

Place the potatoes on the prepared baking sheet, making sure that they are next to each other.

Slide the tray onto the middle rail and bake the potato wedges in the oven for about 30 minutes until golden brown. Be careful not to get too dark. Once done, transfer to a bowl and serve.

POTATO WEDGES MADE FROM SWEET POTATOES

Servings:2

INGREDIENTS

- 3 Pc Sweet potatoes, great
- 3 Tbsp   olive oil
- 1 TL Paprika powder, mild
- 1 TL Ground cumin
- 1 TL Rosemary, finely chopped
- 1 prize   salt

PREPARATION

First preheat the oven to 220 ° C (fan oven 200 ° C).

In the meantime, peel and wash the sweet potatoes. Then cut into corners or crevices and place in an ovenproof dish.

Next, drizzle the olive oil over the sweet potatoes. Scatter the paprika powder, cumin, rosemary and salt on top and mix the potatoes thoroughly with both hands.

Place the dish on the middle rack in the preheated oven and bake the sweet potato wedges for about 30 minutes until they are soft on the inside and crispy on the outside.

POTATO WEDGES FROM THE AIR FRYER

Servings:2

INGREDIENTS

- 600 G   Potatoes, waxy
- 2 TL olive oil
- 1 prize   sea-salt
- 1 prize   Pepper, black, freshly ground
- 0.5 TL   Rosemary, finely chopped
- 0.5 TL   Thyme, dried

For the dip

- 1 Pc   Avocado, ripe
- 2 Tbsp   Natural yoghurt
- 1 TL   Guacamole seasoning

- 1 TL   Lemon juice

PREPARATION

First wash the potatoes thoroughly and brush them off. Then - depending on the size - quarter or eighth.

Then place in a bowl, drizzle with the oil and season with salt, pepper, rosemary and thyme. Mix the potatoes well with these ingredients.

Now set the air fryer to 180 ° C and a cooking time of 20 minutes.

Add the potatoes, after 10 minutes open the deep fryer, mix the potatoes for an evenly browned result and then finish cooking.

During the cooking time, cut open the avocado, remove the stone and scoop out the pulp. Put in a bowl, mash with a fork and mix with the lemon juice, yogurt and guacamole seasoning.

Take the finished potato wedges out of the air fryer and serve with the avocado dip.

MASHED POTATOES WITHOUT BUTTER

Servings:4

INGREDIENTS

- 1   kg Potatoes, floury cooking
- 1 TL   Salt, for the cooking water
- 150 ml   Milk (1.5% fat content)
- 2 Tbsp   Sour cream (10% fat content)
- 1 prize   salt
- 1 prize   Pepper, white, freshly ground
- 1 prize   Nutmeg, freshly grated

PREPARATION

Peel, wash and cut the potatoes into large cubes. Then put in a saucepan, cover with salted water and cook over medium heat for about 20-25 minutes.

Drain the cooked potatoes in a colander and collect the cooking water in a bowl.

Next, heat the milk in a small saucepan for about 3 minutes. Press the potatoes through a potato press and beat the hot milk with a whisk. Then stir in the sour cream.

If the consistency is too firm, stir in some of the potato cooking water that has been collected.

Finally, season the mashed potatoes without butter with salt, nutmeg and pepper and serve immediately.

PAN-FRIED POTATOES

S

Servings: 4

INGREDIENTS

- 30 G Turkey schnitzel, thin
- 3 Tbsp olive oil
- 1 prize salt
- 1 prize Pepper White
- 400 G Potatoes, waxy
- 200 G Mushrooms, small
- 250 G zucchini
- 1 Federation Spring onions
- 250 G broccoli
- 75 G Tomatoes, dried
- 0.5 Federation Parsley, fresh
- 0.5 Federation Oregano, fresh

- 200 G Sour cream

PREPARATION

First wash the turkey escalope, pat dry with kitchen paper and cut into strips.

Then heat a tablespoon of olive oil in a pan and fry the turkey strips brown on all sides. Then season them with salt and pepper, remove from the pan and keep warm.

Now peel, wash and slice the potatoes. Heat the rest of the olive oil in the roasting tray and cover the potatoes for about 20 minutes over a medium heat until they are done - stirring occasionally.

In the meantime, clean the mushrooms and cut them in half. Wash the zucchini and cut into slices. Clean and wash the spring onions and cut into rings.

Add the vegetables to the potatoes after 10 minutes and cook at the same time - season with salt and pepper.

Trim, wash and cut the broccoli into florets. Bring salted water to a boil in a saucepan, cook the broccoli florets in it for 8 minutes, then drain and drain.

Cut the sun-dried tomatoes into small pieces. Then fold the meat, broccoli and tomato pieces into the potatoes, season again with salt and pepper and warm up.

Finally, pluck the parsley and oregano from the stems, wash, shake dry and chop finely. Mix the herbs with the sour cream and serve to the potato and vegetable pan.

POTATO AND VEGETABLE PAN WITH EGG

Servings: 2

INGREDIENTS

- 800 G   Potatoes, waxy
- 200 G Corn (can)
- 6   Pc Eggs
- 80 G Parsley, finely chopped
- 2   Tbsp   Rapeseed oil
- 20 Pc Tomatoes, small
- 1 prize   salt
- 1 prize   pepper

PREPARATION

For the potato and vegetable pan with egg, first carefully peel the waxy potatoes with a potato peeler or knife, wash and bring to the boil in a large saucepan with lightly salted water. Now boil the potatoes for 10 minutes, then carefully drain and cut into slices.

At the same time, heat the rapeseed oil in a shallow pan and fry the potatoes in it for a few minutes.

Wash the tomatoes, dab them with a kitchen towel and then quarter them. Put the canned sweet corn in a sieve, rinse well and allow to drain. Then add the quartered tomatoes and corn to the potatoes and carefully fold in.

Then mix the eggs and a pinch of salt and pepper in a bowl with a whisk and add to the other ingredients in the pan. Mix everything well and let set for 5 minutes. Stir carefully every now and then to avoid burning anything.

POTATO AND PEA PUREE

Servings:4

INGREDIENTS

- 1 kg   Potatoes, floury cooking
- 200 G Peas, young, frozen
- 2 Tbsp   butter
- 1 prize   salt
- 1 prize   Pepper, black, freshly ground
- 1 Msp Nutmeg, freshly grated
- 250 ml   milk

PREPARATION

First peel the potatoes, wash them and cut them into large pieces. Then put in a saucepan, cover with water and cook for about 20 minutes.

In the last 3 minutes of the cooking time, add the frozen peas to the potatoes and cook at the same time. Then pour into a sieve and drain well, then transfer to a saucepan.

Heat the milk in a small saucepan for about 3 minutes. Coarsely mash the potato and pea mixture with a potato masher and pour in the milk until the puree has a creamy consistency.

Now stir the butter into the mashed potatoes and peas, season with salt, pepper and freshly grated nutmeg. Keep the puree warm until serving

CARAMELIZED FENNEL

Servings: 4

INGREDIENTS

- 750 G Fennel bulb
- 5 Pc Shallots
- 1 shot Olive oil for the pan
- 4 Tbsp honey
- 120 ml White wine, dry
- 1 Tbsp Lemon peel, grated (organic)
- 1 prize salt and pepper

PREPARATION

Clean and wash the fennel, cut in the middle and cut out the hard stalk, then slice into fine strips.

Then remove the skin from the shallots and finely chop the shallots.

Now heat the oil in a pan and fry or braise the fennel and shallots in it.

Drizzle the honey over it and let everything caramelize briefly. Pour white wine, add lemon zest and stir in.

Cook the vegetables for about 10 minutes and then season with salt and pepper.

VEAL STOCK OR VEAL BROTH

Servings:10

INGREDIENTS

- 2 kg Calf bones
- 4 Pc Carrots, great
- 2 Pc Onions
- 1 kpf Celeriac, small
- 3 Pc Parsley roots
- 2 Tbsp Vegetable oil, for the vegetables
- 3 Water, cold
- 3 gl Water, for the vegetables

PREPARATION

First preheat the oven to 180 ° C top / bottom heat.

In the meantime, rinse the veal bones with cold water and place them in a wide pot or roasting pan so that all bones touch the bottom of the pot. Then place the pot on the lowest rail in the preheated oven and brown the bones for about 1 hour - without adding any fat.

Meanwhile, wash the carrots, celery and parsley roots and cut into large pieces. Peel the onions and chop them roughly as well. Heat a little vegetable oil in a pan, fry the diced vegetables in it and let them take on a strong color in about 10 minutes.

Then deglaze the roast with 1 glass of water, boil down completely for about 5 minutes and repeat this process 2 more times.

Now take the pot out of the oven, add the roasted vegetables and pour in the water. Bones and vegetables should be covered with about 1 cm of water.

Reduce the temperature to 160 ° C top / bottom heat, let the contents of the pot simmer gently for about 6 hours and skim off the foam in between.

When the cooking time is over, pour the veal stock or veal stock through a fine sieve into a large saucepan and allow to cool. Remove the white layer of fat and use it elsewhere if necessary.

Pour the now slimy stock through a fine sieve again and make sure that no sediment is poured out with it. Use the stock or the stock or freeze it in portions.

STEAMED COD WITH RADISHES

Servings:4

INGREDIENTS

- 900 G Cod fillet
- 1 Federation radish
- 0.7 Federation dill
- 0.5 Federation chives
- 0.5 Pc Lemon, organic
- 1 prize salt
- 1 prize pepper
- 3 Tbsp Horseradish, grated (glass)
- 1 Tbsp olive oil

PREPARATION

First rinse the fish, pat dry with kitchen paper and remove any bones, preferably with tweezers.

Now remove the greens and roots from the radishes, wash them thoroughly and slice them into thin slices.

Wash, dry and finely chop the delicate leaves of radish greens, dill and chives.

Now wash the lemon with hot water, finely dice it together with the peel, then mix with the radishes and herbs.

Then spread out a suitable piece of parchment paper and spread half of the radish and herb mixture on it lengthways. Place the fish fillet on the mixture, season with salt and pepper and brush with horseradish. Then spread the rest of the radish and herb mixture on the fish and seal the parchment cover.

Now place the parcel in a steamer or pot with a steamer insert and steam for about 25 minutes.

Finally, take out the parcel, place on a serving platter, open in the middle and serve the cod steamed with radishes drizzled with olive oil.

COD WITH MUSHROOMS

Servings: 4

INGREDIENTS

- 500 G Cod fillet
- 1 Pc Lemon, juice
- 0.5 TL salt
- 2 TL Rosemary needles
- 1 Tbsp Flour
- 5 Pc spring onions
- 170 G Mushrooms
- 2 Tbsp butter
- 1 prize pepper
- 100 ml White wine
- 1 Tbsp Parsley, chopped
- 1 Tbsp Crème fine

PREPARATION

Wash the fish fillet, pat dry with kitchen paper and cut into bite-sized pieces. Then halve the lemon, squeeze it and sprinkle 1 tablespoon of lemon juice over the fish fillets. Finally, season with salt and sprinkle with flour.

Clean the spring onions, cut into rings, wash and drain. Clean the mushrooms, cut in half and immediately drizzle with lemon juice.

Melt butter in a pan, add washed rosemary needles and season with pepper. Then add the mushrooms and spring onions and cook over medium heat for about 5 minutes.

Then add the pieces of fish, fry for about 6 minutes, deglaze with white wine and season with salt, lemon juice and pepper.

Finally fold in the crème fine and serve sprinkled with parsley.

YOGURT GRANOLA WITH BANANA

Servings:2

INGREDIENTS

- 2 Tbsp   Wheat grains
- 3 TL   Raisins
- 3 TL   Walnuts, chopped
- 1 TL   Wheat bran
- 1 Pc   banana
- 2 Tbsp   Liquid honey
- 300 G Yogurt, low fat
- 60   G Kefir, low fat
- 4   Pc   Walnut kernel halves, to the yarn.

PREPARATION

First, put the wheat grains and raisins in a small saucepan, just cover with water and soak overnight. The next day, drain the water and add the nuts and bran to the pot and mix.

Then peel the banana for the yoghurt muesli with banana , cut one half into thin slices and mash the other half with a fork. Arrange the banana slices on 2 bowls.

Mix the banana puree with the honey in a bowl with the yogurt. Mix in the kefir and cereal mixture.

Finally, distribute the yoghurt mixture between the two bowls and garnish each portion with two walnuts.

YOGURT GARLIC SAUCE

Servings:4

INGREDIENTS

- 1 Bch Skimmed milk yogurt
- 1 TL   Herbal salt
- 1 prize   pepper
- 4   Pc Garlic cloves
- 1   Spr Lemon juice

PREPARATION

First peel the garlic cloves and press them through the garlic press into a bowl. Then mix well with the yogurt.

Finally, season the yoghurt garlic sauce with lemon juice, herb salt and pepper and serve.

YOGHURT HONEY MUSTARD DRESSING

Servings:4

INGREDIENTS

- 200 G   Natural yogurt, more Greek
- 6   TL Honey, liquid
- 4   TL Dijon mustard
- 1   prize   salt
- 1   prize   Pepper, black, freshly ground
- 0.5 Federation   chives

PREPARATION

First put the yogurt in a bowl and stir in the honey with a flat whisk.

Then add the mustard, stir in and season with salt and pepper.

Wash the chives, pat dry and cut into very fine rolls with scissors. Stir the chives rolls into the yogurt honey mustard dressing.

Season the dressing with a pinch of paprika powder and cover and chill.

ITALIAN BREAD SALAD - PANZANELLA

Servings:2

INGREDIENTS

- 300 G   Stale bread (any kind)
- 1 Spr Olive oil (virgin, good quality)
- 2 Pc   Garlic cloves
- 5 Pc   Vine tomatoes
- 2 Pc   Cucumber
- 1 prize   salt
- 1 prize   Pepper (freshly ground)
- 250 mg   Vinegar (red wine vinegar)
- 250 ml   water
- 1 prize   Brown sugar

- 1 Federation basil
- 1 Pc   Onion, red

PREPARATION

First cut the bread into approx. 2 cm cubes and preheat the oven to 140 ° C. Then spread the bread cubes on a tray and drizzle with a little olive oil.

In the next step, press the garlic cloves with their skin on and spread them on the bread. Now toast the bread cubes until they are golden brown.

In the meantime, wash the tomatoes, cut them in half and cut the cucumber into cubes. Finely chop the red onion and place in a bowl, season with salt and let stand for about 10 minutes.

Now add the tomatoes and cucumbers to the onions and season to taste with olive oil, vinegar, water, brown sugar, salt and freshly ground pepper.

Finally add the toasted bread cubes and mix well with the basil leaves. Let the whole thing rest for about 10 minutes and then serve.

ITALIAN ONION SOUP

Servings:4

INGREDIENTS

- 4 TL Parsley, fresh, chopped
- 2 Pc Garlic cloves
- 5 Pc Onions
- 3 Tbsp Olive oil, for the pot
- 300 ml White wine, dry
- 450 ml Vegetable broth, of course
- 1 Tbsp Lemon juice
- 1 TL salt
- 0.5 TL pepper
- 4 Schb White bread, toasted
- 250 G Pecorino, grated
- 0.5 TL sugar

- 1 shot Wine vinegar

PREPARATION

For the Italian onion soup, first peel the onions and cut into rings. Also peel and finely chop the garlic.

Then heat the olive oil in a saucepan and sauté the onion and garlic pieces in it.

Deglaze with the wine and vegetable stock and put the lid on. Simmer for around 10 minutes at a low temperature, add salt, pepper, sugar and season to taste with lemon juice and a dash of wine vinegar.

Using a glass or a cookie cutter, cut out small circles from the white bread (or toasted bread), sprinkle with cheese and bake in the oven at approx. 170 degrees for approx. 10 minutes.

Arrange the onion soup in plates and serve the gratinated toast slices as an insert.

GINGER JAM WITH ORANGES

Servings:4

INGREDIENTS

- 5   Pc Oranges
- 45 ml Orange juice, unsweetened
- 500 G Preserving sugar, 2: 1
- 1   Pc Ginger, fresh (about the size of a thumb)

PREPARATION

Remove the peel from the oranges, divide into segments and fillet - also remove the stones. Weigh the orange fillets and use another 500 grams.

Then peel the ginger and grate finely, then weigh 10 grams of it.

Then stir the orange juice in a saucepan with the orange fillets, the ginger and the preserving sugar, bring to the boil and boil over high heat, stirring constantly (approx. 4 minutes). Skim off the resulting foam.

Then immediately fill the hot ginger jam with oranges into sterilized jars and seal them airtight with a screw cap. Turn upside down and let stand for 5 minutes.

GINGER-LEMON DIP

Servings:4

INGREDIENTS

- 250 G Sour cream or crème fraîche
- 3 cm ginger
- 1 Pc Lemons, juice and peel
- 1 prize salt
- 5 cm Lemongrass

PREPARATION

Peel and finely grate or chop the ginger. Wash the lemongrass, shake it dry and also chop it very finely.

Then mix both in a bowl with the juice and the grated zest of the lemon.

Finally, stir in the sour cream and season the ginger-lemon dip with salt.

INDIAN PRAWN CURRY

Servings: 4

INGREDIENTS

- 1 Tbsp turmeric
- 1.5 TL Coriander, ground
- 2 Tbsp Coriander, fresh
- 1 TL cumin
- 1 prize nutmeg
- 1 Pc Ginger, fresh, about 5 cm
- 3 Pc Garlic cloves
- 2 Pc Onions
- 3 Tbsp peanut oil
- 400 G Tomato pieces (Tetra Pack)
- 200 ml water
- 5 Tbsp Lemon juice

- 5 Pc   Curry leaves
- 800 G Prawns, fresh
- 1 Stg cinnamon
- 1 prize   Chilli powder

PREPARATION

First mix the turmeric, coriander, cumin, chili powder and nutmeg in a bowl.

Then peel the ginger and rub it with the spices in the bowl. Peel the garlic, press it through a garlic press and add. Then add 5 tablespoons of water and stir to make a paste.

Peel and finely chop the onions and sauté in a pan with hot oil until translucent.

Then stir in the spice paste, simmer for 1 minute, then add the tomato pieces, pour in the water and add lemon juice, cinnamon stick and curry leaves. Now let the whole thing simmer over a mild heat for about 30 minutes.

In the meantime, wash the prawns, pat dry with kitchen paper and add to the curry 4 minutes before serving. Then remove the cinnamon stick and the curry leaves again.

Wash the coriander greens, shake dry, chop finely and serve the Indian prawn curry sprinkled with it.

CHICKEN FILLET WITH MUSHROOMS AND PARSLEY

Servings:4

INGREDIENTS

- 1 prize   salt
- 2 Tbsp   Parsley (fresh)
- 2 Tbsp   oil
- 2 Tbsp   Flour
- 2 Pc   garlic
- 750 ml   Vegetable broth
- 800 G   Chicken fillet
- 200 G Mushrooms
- 1 Pc   onion
- 1 prize   pepper

- 1 shot cream

PREPARATION

First peel and chop the onion. Heat the oil in a pan, then roast the onion pieces in it, dust with flour and add the vegetable stock.

Wash the parsley, shake dry, chop and add. Clean, wash, slice and add the mushrooms.

Remove the skin and tendons from the chicken fillet, then rinse with water, pat dry, cut into small pieces and mix in. Now let the whole thing simmer for about 10-15 minutes.

Just before serving, refine with a little cream and, if necessary, thicken with a sauce thickener. Season with salt and pepper.

ITALIAN STYLE CHICKEN BREAST STRIPS

Servings:4

INGREDIENTS

- 600 G   Chicken breast fillets
- 1 prize   salt
- 2 Tbsp   Olive oil, for the pan
- 1 prize   pepper

For the tomato sauce

- 300 G   Tomatoes, peeled (tin)
- 4 Pc Garlic cloves
- 1 Pc onion
- 1 prize   salt
- 1 prize   pepper

- 1 TL   sugar
- 1 shot Vegetable broth

PREPARATION

Wash the chicken, pat dry with kitchen paper, remove the skin and tendons, cut into strips approx. 1 cm thick and season with salt and pepper.

Heat olive oil in a pan and fry the chicken strips on both sides for a few minutes. Then take the meat out of the pan and keep it warm.

For the tomato sauce, peel the garlic and onions, chop them finely and roast them briefly in the roast.

Then add the peeled tomatoes, season with salt, pepper and sugar, add a little vegetable stock if necessary and let it simmer for a few minutes.

Then strain the tomato sauce (= strain through a sieve) and serve with the chicken breast strips.

MILLET PORRIDGE WITH GRAPES

Servings:1

INGREDIENTS

- 700 ml   milk
- 1 prize   salt
- 100 G Organic millet flakes
- 1 Pa   Grapes
- 1 TL   vanilla sugar
- 1 Tbsp   honey

PREPARATION

For the millet porridge, first put the milk in a saucepan, bring to the boil together with the millet and simmer for around 15-20 minutes on a low heat - stirring occasionally.

Then season the millet porridge with a pinch of salt, vanilla sugar and, if you like, a little honey.

Pour the mash into a bowl, cut or halve the grapes and spread over the mash. If necessary, sprinkle a little with ground cinnamon or cocoa powder.

MILLET COMPOTE WITH APPLE AND CINNAMON

Servings:4

INGREDIENTS

- 1 Pc   lemon
- 250 G millet
- soy milk
- 7 Tbsp   Agave syrup
- 3 Pc   Apples
- 1 TL   Ground cinnamon
- 30 G almonds
- 100 G Natural yoghurt

PREPARATION

First rinse the millet with warm water through a sieve and drain well.

Then heat the soy milk in a saucepan over medium heat and stir in 5 tablespoons of the agave syrup.

Then add the millet and let the whole swell (do not boil) for 20 minutes, stirring occasionally.

In the meantime, peel, core and stalk the apples and cut into small cubes.

Then wash and dry the lemon and finely rub the peel with a kitchen grater. Now halve the lemon and squeeze out.

Next, bring the lemon juice together with the remaining 2 tablespoons of agave syrup to a boil over high heat and add the apples and cinnamon. Heat the whole thing over medium heat for another 5 minutes.

In the next step, roast the almond slivers in a pan without oil for 5 minutes over medium heat until golden brown.

Then mix the millet into the apple and cinnamon mixture and also the yoghurt.

Finally, pour the almonds over the millet compote with apple and cinnamon and serve.

HOT GAZPACHO

Servings:4

INGREDIENTS

- 1 Pc   onion
- 1 Pc   Paprika, yellow
- 1 Pc   Paprika, red
- 200 G zucchini
- 200 G Tomato pieces (TetraPack)
- 2 Tbsp   olive oil
- 1 Tbsp   Thyme, chopped
- 450 ml   Vegetable broth
- 25 G ginger
- 100 ml   Creme fraiche Cheese
- 4 Tbsp   Lemon juice
- 0.5 TL   Sambal Oelek

- 1 Pc   clove of garlic

PREPARATION

Halve the peppers, remove the core, wash and cut into cubes. Wash the zucchini and cut into small pieces. Set aside some of the diced vegetables for the garnish.

Peel onion and garlic and chop finely.

Heat the oil in a saucepan and sauté the onion and garlic pieces in it. Then add the thyme and the roughly chopped pepper and zucchini pieces, fry briefly and then stir in the tomatoes. Then pour the vegetable stock on top, put the lid on and let simmer for 15 minutes on a low level.

Then puree the soup finely and strain through a sieve into another saucepan. Peel the ginger, dice it finely, add it to the soup together with the crème fraîche and bring it to the boil again.

Finally, season the hot gazpacho with sambal oelek and lemon juice, divide into soup bowls, sprinkle with the vegetables you have set aside and serve sprinkled with a little parsley.

HARE WITH HUNTER SAUCE

Servings:4

INGREDIENTS

- 5 Tbsp   Sunflower oil
- 2 Tbsp   Clarified butter
- 1 Tbsp   cognac
- 5 Schb   Bacon, mixed
- 150 G Mushrooms
- 5 Tbsp   Vegetable broth
- 1 Pc   Rabbit, disassembled
- 1 Pc   clove of garlic
- 1 Pc   Lemon, juice
- 3 Pc   tomatoes
- 1 prize   salt and pepper
- 1 Tbsp   Flour

PREPARATION

Peel the garlic and press it through the garlic press. Squeeze the lemon and collect the juice.

For the marinade, mix the oil, garlic, and lemon juice, salt and pepper together. Rub and pour over the rabbit pieces and marinate for at least 4 hours.

Clean the mushrooms and cut into pieces of equal size (halve or quarter).

Scald tomatoes with hot water, peel them and cut into small pieces

Drain the meat in a sieve while collecting the marinade. Pat the rabbit pieces dry with kitchen paper.

Melt the clarified butter in a casserole and fry the strips of bacon over medium heat until they are light brown. Add the pieces of hare and fry for about 30 minutes over low heat, turning the pieces frequently.

Pour in the vegetable stock, cognac and the marinade. Add the mushrooms and tomatoes and cover and let simmer for another 40 minutes over a low heat.

Remove pieces of hare, season to taste and thicken with flour.

HAND CHEESE WITH MUSIC

Servings: 3

INGREDIENTS

- 3 Pc   Hand cheese
- 1 prize   pepper
- 1 prize   salt
- 1 prize   Caraway seed
- 1 shot   Wine vinegar
- 1 Bch   Cider
- 2 Tbsp   oil
- 1 Pc   Onion, small
- 1 prize   Parsley, chopped
- 1 Schb   Onion, red

PREPARATION

First, take the hand cheese out of the packaging, place it in a sealable bowl and pour the oil over it until it shines slightly.

Now pour in the cider and a dash of wine vinegar and marinate the hand cheese in it.

Add a little salt and pepper to taste.

The addition of a little caraway makes the dish easier on the stomach.

For the "music" peel the onions, cut into very small cubes and sprinkle over the cheese.

Now close the can with the lid, turn it upside down and shake a little so that all the ingredients mix well.

Soak the hand cheese in the refrigerator for 6 hours and let it rest.

Then arrange the cheese on 3 plates, pour the stock over them and serve sprinkled with parsley.

GRUEL

Servings:2

INGREDIENTS

- 200 G Oatmeal, fine
- 1 prize   salt
- 1 Tbsp   sugar
- 400 ml   milk
- 1 prize   Ground cinnamon
- 1 TL vanilla sugar

PREPARATION

Put the milk together with the oat flakes, a pinch of salt, sugar and vanilla sugar in a saucepan and bring to the boil briefly. Stir constantly so that the gruel does not burn.

Then take the pot off the hotplate and let it soak for a good 5 minutes with the lid closed.

Then fill the gruel in small bowls and serve sprinkled with sugar and cinnamon.

OAT GROATS WITH BANANAS

Servings:2

INGREDIENTS

- 100   Goatmeal
- 300 ml   water
- 1 prize   salt
- 2 Pc banana
- 50 G Fruit mix, dried

PREPARATION

First peel the banana and cut it into small slices. Then bring hot water, oat flakes and salt to the boil in a saucepan and simmer for 5 minutes on a low flame. Always stir so that the mixture becomes creamy.

Just before the end of the cooking time, stir in the fruit mix and simmer briefly. Pour the mixture into bowls and spread the banana slices over them.

OATMEAL DRINK

Servings:2

INGREDIENTS

- 200 G Natural or fruit yogurt
- 1 Pc   Banana, great
- 4 Tbsp   Oatmeal, hearty
- 100 ml   orange juice

PREPARATION

For this healthy drink, pour the natural yogurt into a tall mug. (If you don't like so much nature, just take fruit yoghurt.)

Then take a banana out of the skin and cut it into pieces. Put these pieces with the oatmeal in the mug with the yogurt.

Then finely puree the whole thing, preferably with a hand blender.

If the drink is a bit too thick, just add orange juice.

Finally, divide the oatmeal drink between 2 glasses and serve.

CHICKEN BREAST STRIPS WITH PAPRIKA

Servings: 2

INGREDIENTS

- 2 Pc Bell pepper, red
- 1 Pc clove of garlic
- 400 G Chicken breast fillet
- 1 cm Ginger, fresh
- 2 between Thyme, fresh
- 4 Tbsp Rapeseed oil
- 1 prize salt
- 1 prize Pepper, freshly ground
- 50 ml Vegetable broth

PREPARATION

First cut the peppers in half, remove the core and core, wash under running water and cut into strips.

Then peel and finely chop the garlic. Peel, wash and finely grate the ginger. Wash the thyme sprigs, shake dry, pluck the leaves off and chop finely.

Remove skin and tendons from the chicken breast fillets, rinse under cold water, pat dry with kitchen paper, cut into strips and season with salt and pepper.

Now heat 2 tablespoons of oil in a pan and fry the chicken breast strips all around for 5 minutes until golden brown. Then remove from the pan and set aside.

Heat 2 tablespoons of oil in the pan again, then sauté the pepper strips, garlic and ginger over medium heat for 3 minutes. Then add the thyme, salt, pepper and then deglaze with the vegetable stock. Steam the vegetables for 5 minutes.

Now put the chicken breast strips back into the pan, fold them under the vegetables and continue to fry for 4 minutes.

CHICKEN BREAST SALAD

S

Servings:4

INGREDIENTS

- 2 Pc Chicken breast fillet, grilled
- 3 Stg Celeriac
- 2 Pc Carrots
- 5 Pc spring onions
- 2 tbsp Flaked almonds

for the marinade

- 2 Tbsp Raisins
- 3 cl Sherry, medium dry
- 1 prize salt and pepper
- 5 Tbsp olive oil
- 1 prize Cayenne pepper

- 1 shot White wine vinegar

PREPARATION

First heat about 50 ml of water, add it to the raisins, then pour off the water, dry the raisins with kitchen paper, put them in a cup, pour the sherry over them and let them steep.

In the meantime, cut the grilled chicken breast fillets into bite-sized pieces.

Scrape the carrots and slice into thin sticks. If necessary, peel off the coarse threads from the celery, wash the celery and cut into small pieces. Clean the spring onions, remove the roots, wash and cut the spring onions into rings. Then put the meat, carrots, celery and spring onions in a bowl.

For the marinade, mix vinegar with salt and pepper. Stir the raisins with the sherry and olive oil into the vinegar and season with cayenne pepper.

Then pour the marinade over the salad ingredients, mix well and serve the chicken breast salad garnished with the almond flakes.

CONCLUSION

If you want to lose a few pounds, the low-carb and low-fat diet will eventually reach your limits. Although the weight can be reduced with the diets, the success is usually only short-lived because the diets are too one-sided. So if you want to lose weight and avoid a classic yo-yo effect, you should rather check your energy balance and recalculate your daily calorie requirement.

The ideal is to adhere to a gentle variant of the low-fat diet with 60 to 80 grams of fat per day for life. It helps to maintain the weight and protects against diabetes and high blood lipids with all their health risks.

The low-fat diet is comparably easy to implement because you only have to forego fatty foods or severely limit their proportion of the daily amount of food. With the low-carb diet, on the other hand, much more precise planning and more stamina are necessary. Anything that really fills you up is usually high in carbohydrates and should be avoided. Under certain circumstances, this can lead to food cravings and thus to failure of the diet. It is essential that you eat properly. Many statutory health insurance companies therefore offer prevention courses or pay you for individual nutritional advice. Such advice is extremely important, especially if you decide on a weight-loss diet in which you want to permanently change your entire diet. Whether your private health insurance pays for such measures depends on the tariff you have taken out. In the meantime, however, individual nutritional advice has been taken over by many private provi

LOW-FAT COOKBOOK

A Low Fat Cookbook with Over 50 Quick & Easy Recipes

Karen Ward

All rights reserved.

Disclaimer

The information contained i is meant to serve as a comprehensive collection of strategies that the author of this eBook has done research about. Summaries, strategies, tips and tricks are only recommendation by the author, and reading this eBook will not guarantee that one's results will exactly mirror the author's results. The author of the eBook has made all reasonable effort to provide current and accurate information for the readers of the eBook. The author and it's associates will not be held liable for any unintentional error or omissions that may be found. The material in the eBook may include information by third parties. Third party materials comprise of opinions expressed by their owners. As such, the author of the eBook does not assume responsibility or liability for any third party material or opinions. Whether because of the progression of the internet, or the unforeseen changes in company policy and editorial submission guidelines, what is stated as fact at the time of this writing may become outdated or inapplicable later.

The eBook is copyright © 2021 with all rights reserved. It is illegal to redistribute, copy, or create derivative work from this eBook whole or in part. No parts of this report may be reproduced or retransmitted in any reproduced or retransmitted in any forms whatsoever without the writing expressed and signed permission from the author

INTRODUCTION

A low-fat diet reduces the amount of fat that is ingested through food, sometimes drastically. Depending on how extreme this diet or nutrition concept is implemented, a mere 30 grams of fat may be consumed per day.

With conventional wholefood nutrition according to the interpretation of the German Nutrition Society, the recommended value is more than twice as high (approx. 66 grams or 30 to 35 percent of the daily energy intake). By greatly reducing dietary fat, the pounds should drop and / or not sit back on the hips.

Even if there are no prohibited foods per se with this diet: With liver sausage, cream and French fries you have reached the daily limit for fat faster than you can say "far from full". Therefore, for a low-fat diet, mainly or exclusively foods with a low fat content should end up on the plate - preferably "good" fats such as those in fish and vegetable oils.

WHAT ARE THE BENEFITS OF A LOW-FAT DIET?

Fat provides vital (essential) fatty acids. The body also needs fat to be able to absorb certain vitamins (A, D, E, K) from food. Eliminating fat in your diet altogether would therefore not be a good idea.

In fact, especially in wealthy industrial nations, significantly more fat is consumed every day than is recommended by experts. One problem with this is that fat is particularly rich in energy - one gram of it contains 9.3 calories and thus twice as many as one gram of carbohydrates or protein. An increased intake of fat therefore promotes obesity. In addition, too many saturated fatty acids, such as those in butter, lard or chocolate, are said to increase the risk of cardiovascular diseases and even cancer. Eating low-fat diets could prevent both of these problems.

LOW FAT FOODS: TABLE FOR LEAN ALTERNATIVES

Most people should be aware that it is not healthy to stuff yourself into uncontrolled fat. Obvious sources of fat such as fat rims on meat and sausage or butter lakes in the frying pan are easy to avoid.

It becomes more difficult with hidden fats, such as those found in pastries or cheese. With the latter, the amount of fat is sometimes given as an absolute percentage, sometimes as "% FiTr.", I.e. the fat content in the dry matter that arises when the water is removed from the food .

For a low-fat diet you have to look carefully, because a cream quark with 11.4% fat sounds lower in fat than one with 40% FiTr .. Both products have the same fat content. Lists from nutrition experts (e.g. the DGE) help to integrate a low-fat diet into everyday life as easily as possible and to avoid tripping hazards. For example, here is an instead of a table (high-fat foods with low-fat alternatives):

High fat foods

Low fat alternatives

Butter

Cream cheese, herb quark, mustard, sour cream, tomato paste

French fries, fried potatoes, croquettes, potato pancakes

Jacket potatoes, baked potatoes or baked potatoes

Pork belly, sausage, goose, duck

Veal, venison, turkey, pork cutlet, -lende, chicken, duck breast without skin

Lyoner, mortadella, salami, liver sausage, black pudding, bacon

Cooked / smoked ham without a fat rim, low-fat sausages such as salmon ham, turkey breast, roast meats, aspic sausage

Fat-free alternatives to sausage or cheese or to combine with them

Tomato, cucumber, radish slices, lettuce on bread or even banana slices / thin apple wedges, strawberries

Fish sticks

Steamed, low-fat fish

Tuna, salmon, mackerel, herring

Steamed cod, saithe, haddock

Milk, yoghurt (3.5% fat)

Milk, yoghurt (1.5% fat)

Cream quark (11.4% fat = 40% FiTr.)

Quark (5.1% fat = 20% FiTr.)

Double cream cheese (31.5% fat)

Layered cheese (2.0% fat = 10% FiTr.)

Fat cheese (> 15% fat = 30% FiTr.)

Low-fat cheeses (max. 15% fat = max. 30% FiTr.)

Creme fraiche (40% fat)

Sour cream (10% fat)

Mascarpone (47.5% fat)

Grainy cream cheese (2.9% fat)

Fruit cake with short crust pastry

Fruit cake with yeast or sponge batter

Sponge cake, cream cake, chocolate chip cookies, shortbread, chocolate, bars

Low-fat sweets such as Russian bread, ladyfingers, dried fruits, gummy bears, fruit gums, mini chocolate kisses (attention: sugar!)

Nut nougat cream, chocolate slices

Grainy cream cheese with a little jam

Croissants

Pretzel croissants, whole meal rolls, yeast pastries

Nuts, potato chips

Salt sticks or pretzels

Ice cream

Fruit ice cream

Black olives (35.8% fat)

green olives (13.3% fat)

LOW-FAT DIET: HOW TO SAVE FAT IN THE HOUSEHOLD

In addition to exchanging ingredients, there are a few other tricks you can use to incorporate a low-fat diet into your everyday life:

Steaming, stewing and grilling are fat-saving cooking methods for a low-fat diet.

Cook in the Römertopf or with special stainless steel pots. Food can also be prepared without fat in coated pans or in the foil.

You can also save fat with a pump sprayer: fill in about half of the oil and water, shake it and spray it on the base of the cookware before frying. If you don't have a pump sprayer, you can grease the cookware with a brush - this also saves fat.

For a low-fat diet in cream sauces or casseroles, replace half of the cream with milk.

Let soups and sauces cool down and then scoop the fat off the surface.

Prepare sauces with a little oil, sour cream or milk.

Roast and vegetable stocks can be tied with pureed vegetables or grated raw potatoes for a low-fat diet.

Put parchment paper or foil on the baking sheet, then there is no need to grease.

Just add a small piece of butter and fresh herbs to vegetable dishes, and the eyes will soon eat too.

Tie cream dishes with gelatin.

LOW FAT DIET: HOW HEALTHY IS IT REALLY?

For a long time, nutrition experts have been convinced that a low-fat diet is the key to a slim figure and health. Butter, cream and red meat, on the other hand, were considered a danger to the heart, blood values and scales. However, more and more studies suggest that fat isn't actually as bad as it gets. In contrast to a reduced-fat nutrition plan, test subjects could, for example, stick to a Mediterranean menu with lots of vegetable oil and fish, were healthier and still did not get fat.

When comparing different studies on fat, American researchers found that there was no connection between the consumption of saturated fat and the risk of coronary heart disease. There was also no clear scientific evidence that low-fat diets prolong life. Only so-called trans fats , which are produced, among other things, during deep-frying and the partial hardening of vegetable fats (in french fries, chips, ready-made baked goods etc.), were classified as dangerous by the scientists.

Those who only or mainly eat low-fat or fat-free foods probably eat more consciously overall, but run the risk of getting too little of the "good fats". There is also a risk of a lack of fat-soluble vitamins, which our body needs fat to absorb.

Low-fat diet: the bottom line

A low-fat diet requires dealing with the foods that one intends to consume. As a result, one is likely to be more conscious of buying, cooking and eating.

For weight loss, however, it is not primarily where the calories come from that counts, but that you take in less of them per day than you use. Even more: (Essential) fats are necessary for general health, since without them the body cannot utilize certain nutrients and cannot carry out certain metabolic processes.

In summary, this means: a low-fat diet can be an effective means of weight control or one to compensate for fat indulgence. It is not advisable to do without dietary fat entirely.

ZUCCHINI SALAD

Serevings:2

INGREDIENTS

- 1   Pc   zucchini
- 1   Pc   Apple
- 2   Pc Spring onion
- 1 prize   salt
- 2 Tbsp Mint, fresh

PREPARATION

Roughly grate the cleaned and washed zucchini in a bowl and season with salt. Let it steep a little and pour off the resulting water.

Then peel the apple and grate with the zucchini. Wash and clean the onion and cut into rings. Finally mix in the chopped mint into the salad.

ZUCCHINI DRESSING

S

Serevings:2

INGREDIENTS

- 3 Tbsp   Sour cream
- 2 Tbsp   Mayonnaise, low fat
- 2 Tbsp   Zucchini, grated
- 2 Tbsp   Onion, grated
- 1 prize   salt

PREPARATION

Finely grate the washed zucchini and peeled onion in a bowl. Then mix in the mayonnaise and sour cream and season well with salt and pepper.

WATERMELON SALAD WITH FETA

Serevings:4

INGREDIENTS

- 1   Pc Watermelon
- 1   Pc Cucumber
- 150   G Feta cheese
- 1   Federation Mint, fresh

for the dressing

- 2 Tbsp   honey
- 1   Pc Lime, the juice of it
- 1 prize   salt

PREPARATION

For this fruity salad, first halve and quarter the watermelon, remove the pulp from the skin and then cut into cubes.

Roughly chop the feta, wash the mint leaves and cut into small pieces. Wash the cucumber, remove the stalk and cut into small pieces.

Then put the melon pieces together with the feta, pieces of cucumber and mint leaves in a bowl and mix well.

For the dressing, mix the honey with the lime juice and salt and pour over the salad.

WHOLE FOOD CASSEROLE WITH POTATOES AND TOMATOES

Serevings:4

INGREDIENTS

- 750 G		Potatoes, waxy
- 2 l	Water, for boiling the potatoes
- 1.5 TL Salt, for cooking the potatoes
- 750 G tomatoes
- 2 Tbsp		Gomasio, sesame salt
- 1 Pc onion
- 1 Pc clove of garlic
- 1 Tbsp		margarine
- 2 Tbsp		Basil, dried
- 100 G Flaked almonds
- 1 Tbsp		Margarine, for the mold

PREPARATION

First peel the potatoes, wash them, cut them into slices, cook them in a saucepan with salted water for about 10 minutes and then drain the water.

In the meantime, wash the tomatoes, remove the buds and cut into slices about the same thickness as the potato slices.

Then peel the onion and garlic and cut into fine cubes.

Melt the margarine (or butter) in a pan and sauté the onion and garlic pieces over low heat for about 5 minutes.

Now grease a casserole dish with margarine and put in the tomato and potato slices in alternating layers; Sprinkle each layer with a little Gomasio. Now preheat the oven to 220 ° C top and bottom heat.

Then distribute the steamed pieces of onion and garlic bellies as well as the basil and flaked almonds evenly over the casserole.

Finally, bake the whole casserole with potatoes and tomatoes in the preheated oven for about 10 minutes.

WHOLE GRAIN STICKS

S

Serevings:1

INGREDIENTS

- 320 G   Whole wheat flour
- 0.5 Pk baking powder
- 1 TL salt
- 140 G lowfat quark
- 7 Tbsp   Sunflower oil
- 5 Tbsp   milk
- 3 Tbsp   Milk for brushing

PREPARATION

Put whole wheat flour, baking powder and salt in a bowl, mix and mix with the quark, oil and milk to a smooth dough.

Now shape the dough into a roll and cut 40 equal pieces with a knife. Shape each piece of dough into a thin, long stick.

Place these on a baking sheet lined with baking paper and brush with milk.

The whole grain Stangerl in a preheated oven at 180 ° C (hot air) (only one plate) Bake about 20 minutes.

VEGETARIAN POINTED CABBAGE STEW

Serevings:4

INGREDIENTS

- 1 kg cabbage
- 300 G Potatoes, mostly waxy, small
- 2 Pc Onions
- 1 Stg Leeks, leeks
- 2 Tbsp Rapeseed oil, for the pot
- 1 l Vegetable broth, unsalted

For spices

- 2 Pc Garlic cloves
- 2 Tbsp sea-salt
- 0.5 TL Pepper, white, freshly ground
- 0.5 TL Nutmeg, freshly grated

- 1 TL Fennel seeds
- 1 TL Cumin seeds
- 1 Pc Cinnamon stick, small
- 1 Pc Bay leaf
- 1 prize   Sea salt, to taste

PREPARATION

Peel and finely dice the onions and garlic. Clean the leek, slit lengthways, wash thoroughly and dice.

Then quarter the pointed cabbage lengthways, remove the stalk and cut the cabbage into bite-sized pieces. Peel and wash the potatoes and cut into 2 cm cubes.

Heat the rapeseed oil in a large saucepan and sweat the onion and garlic cubes in it for about 3-4 minutes.

Then add the pointed cabbage, potatoes and leek. Then season with sea salt, pepper and nutmeg and add the fennel seeds, caraway seeds, cinnamon stick and bay leaf and sauté briefly.

Now pour in the vegetable stock and simmer the vegetarian pointed cabbage stew over low heat for about 25 minutes.

Finally fish out the bay leaf and the cinnamon stick. Season the stew with sea salt again and serve hot.

VEGETARIAN SOLYANKA

S

Serevings:2

INGREDIENTS

- 200 G   Smoked tofu
- 2   Pc Paprika, red and yellow
- 2 Pc   Onions
- 200 G   Tomato paste
- 6   Pc gherkins
- 150 ml   Pickle water
- 800 ml   Vegetable broth, hot
- 1 TL   Cane sugar, brown sugar
- 1   TL Lemon juice
- 1   TL Paprika powder, hot as rose
- 1 prize   Pepper, black, ground
- 125 ml   Whipped cream or soy cream

- 1 prize   salt
- 2 Tbsp   Parsley, chopped
- 5 Tbsp   Rapeseed oil

PREPARATION

Halve, core, wash the peppers and cut into small cubes. Also cut the smoked tofu into cubes.

Peel the onions and chop them into fine pieces. Cut the pickles into small pieces.

Next, heat the rapeseed oil in a saucepan and fry the tofu cubes in it for about 6-8 minutes until crispy and brown.

Then add the onion and pepper cubes to the tofu and fry for about 5 minutes. Add 140 grams of the tomato paste and roast for 1 minute.

Now pour in the vegetable broth, add the pickled cucumbers, the pickled cucumber water and the remaining tomato paste and bring to the boil for 1 minute.

Then season the vegetarian solyanka with salt, pepper, cane sugar and paprika powder and simmer at a low temperature for about 45-55 minutes.

Season the finished soup with whipped cream and lemon juice and add the chopped parsley just before serving.

VEGAN CHILLI

S

Serevings:4

INGREDIENTS

- 120   G Soy granules
- 500 ml   Vegetable broth, hot
- 3 Tbsp   Rapeseed oil
- 2   Pc Onions
- 0.5   TL   Paprika powder, hot
- 0.5 TL   Chilli flakes
- 1 Pc   clove of garlic
- 50   G Tomato paste
- 1 Can Tomatoes, á 400 g
- 250   G Kidney beans
- 1 Can   Corn, á 400 g
- 1 TL   salt

- 1 TL   sugar
- 0.5 TL   Pepper, black, ground

PREPARATION

First heat the vegetable stock and soak the soy granules in it for about 8-10 minutes. Then pour into a sieve, collect the broth and allow the granules to drain well.

Meanwhile, peel and finely dice the onion and garlic. Heat the oil in a shallow saucepan and fry the soy granules with the onion cubes for about 5 minutes.

Then stir in the tomato paste and roast for 1 minute. Stir in garlic, paprika and chilli flakes.

Now drain the beans and corn and add with the tomatoes and the broth and simmer the vegan chilli over low heat for about 20-25 minutes.

Finally, season with salt, pepper and sugar, bring to the boil for 1 minute and serve.

VEGAN TOMATO DIP

s

Serevings:8

INGREDIENTS

- 15 Tbsp   Tomato paste
- 15 Tbsp   Apple Cider Vinegar
- 250 G sugar
- 1 prize   salt
- 1 prize   pepper

PREPARATION

First take a small saucepan, add tomato paste, vinegar and sugar and bring to the boil while stirring on a medium heat.

Then let everything cool down, season with salt and pepper and serve in a bowl.

VEGAN MANGO LASSI

S

Serevings:2

- **INGREDIENTS**
- 1 Pc ripe mango
- 300 G Lupine yogurt
- 150 ml   water
- 1 Tbsp   Agave syrup

PREPARATION

Peel the ripe mango, remove the pulp from the stone and then cut into large pieces.

Put the mango pieces together with the lupine yogurt, water and agave syrup in a blender and puree them finely.

The vegan mango lassi stuffed as desired with ice cubes into glasses and garnish with fresh herbs.

VEGAN STOCK POT

S

Serevings:4

INGREDIENTS

- 4 Pc Eggplant
- 2 Pc Chili peppers, red
- 4 Pc clove of garlic
- 4   Pc Bay leaf
- 4 Pc Paprika, colorful
- 1 Pc   onion
- 750 ml   Vegetable broth
- 2 Tbsp   olive oil
- 1 prize   salt
- 1 prize   Pepper from the grinder
- 1 prize   Paprika powder, hot as rose
- 300 G Potatoes

PREPARATION

First peel the onion and the garlic cloves and chop them into fine pieces. Then wash the eggplants and cut them into slices. Halve, core, wash and cut the bell pepper into strips.

Core, wash and cut the chilli peppers into small pieces. Peel the potatoes and cut into small cubes.

Now heat the olive oil in a saucepan over a medium flame and roast the onion and garlic cubes in it.

Then add the aubergine slices, paprika strips and the chilli pieces and also sauté briefly.

Now add the bay leaves and the potato cubes, pour in the vegetable stock and cook on a low heat for about 25 minutes.

Depending on your taste, season the vegan vegetable pot with salt, pepper and paprika powder and serve.

VEGAN FROZEN YOGURT

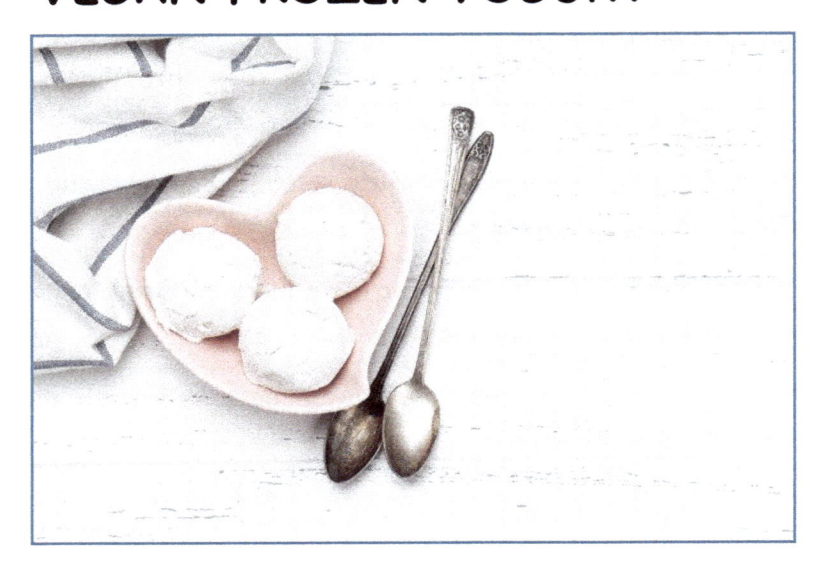

S

Serevings:4

INGREDIENTS

- 6 Tbsp   Maple syrup
- 6 Tbsp   Oat cuisine
- 400 G vegan yogurt (of your choice)
- 4 Tbsp   Oat drink

PREPARATION

To start, add the vegan yogurt, oat drink, maple syrup and coconut milk to the blender.

Mix everything well for one minute and then put in the ice cream maker for 40 minutes.

Finally, put the ice in a freezer and let it set in the freezer for at least 20 minutes.

VEGAN CREAM CHEESE MADE FROM CASHEW NUTS

Serevings:5

INGREDIENTS

- 250 G — Cashew nuts, natural
- 2 Tbsp — Yeast flakes (from Rapunzel)
- 4 Tbsp — Apple Cider Vinegar
- 2 Tbsp — Lemon juice, from the bottle or straight
- 1 prize — salt and pepper
- 0.5 Federation — Chives, fresh

PREPARATION

To start, put the cashews in a large bowl and fill it with enough water to cover the kernels. Now let the whole thing soak overnight.

Then drain the cashew nuts and blend them together with yeast flakes, apple cider vinegar, lemon juice, water, salt and pepper in a blender for about a minute.

Meanwhile wash, dry and finely chop the chives. Then mix the mixer mass with the chives in a bowl, season the whole thing with salt and pepper again and the vegan cream cheese made from cashew nuts is ready .

VEGAN MUSHROOM SPREAD

S

Serevings:4

INGREDIENTS

- 200 G Mushrooms
- 2 Pc Onions
- 100 ml Soy cream
- 0.25 TL salt
- 0.25 TL pepper
- 2 Tbsp Chives, chopped
- 2 Tbsp Yeast flakes
- 1 Tbsp Lemon juice
- 1 shot olive oil
- 1 Tbsp Almond butter

PREPARATION

To start, heat the olive oil in a pan, clean the mushrooms, cut into thin slices and fry in the pan with the olive oil for about 10 minutes until all the liquid has evaporated.

Meanwhile, peel the onions, cut into cubes and place in a bowl with soy cream, almond butter and lemon juice.

Then take the mushrooms out of the pan, add them to the bowl and add the yeast flakes, salt, pepper and chives.

Finally, put all the ingredients in a blender and mix the vegan mushroom spread to a creamy mass

VEGAN SPREAD WITH BEETROOT AND HORSERADISH

Serevings:8

INGREDIENTS

- 100 G Sweet lupins, ground
- 2 Tbsp Tahini (sesame mushroom)
- 4 Tbsp olive oil
- 1 TL Lemon juice
- 1 prize salt
- 1 prize pepper
- 1 Kn Beetroot, pre-cooked
- 1 TL Cream horseradish

PREPARATION

First prepare the crushed sweet lupins according to the instructions on the packet.

Then let the lupins cool down a little and finely puree them with tahini, olive oil and lemon juice. Then season with salt and pepper.

Peel the beetroot, cut into large pieces, add to the lupins together with the horseradish and puree again.

Finally , fill the vegan spread with beetroot and horseradish into a clean, sealable glass and store in the refrigerator.

VEGAN OVERNIGHT OATS WITH STRAWBERRIES

Serevings:4

INGREDIENTS

- 200 G   oatmeal
- 500 ml   Almond milk
- 500 G Strawberries
- 4 TL honey

PREPARATION

Mix the oat flakes with almond milk the evening before and leave to swell overnight in the refrigerator.

The next morning, divide the overnight oats into four glasses. Wash, dry and quarter fresh strawberries.

Fold 3/4 of the mixture from the strawberries into the overnight oats and use 1/4 for decoration.

Finally, drizzle the overnight oats with honey if desired.

VEGAN MOUSSAKA

S

Serevings:4

INGREDIENTS

- 300 G   Potatoes, waxy
- 400 G aubergine
- 300 G zucchini
- 2 Pc Tomatoes, great
- 0.5 TL   Salt, for the cooking water
- 1 Tbsp   Olive oil, for the shape
- 1 prize   salt
- for the tomato sauce
- 2 Pc Garlic cloves
- 2 Pc Shallots
- 3 Tbsp   olive oil
- 2 Tbsp   Tomato paste

- 400 G Tomatoes, chopped, can
- 1 prize   sugar
- 400 ml   Vegetable broth, hot
- 2 TL Thyme leaves, chopped
- 1 TL Paprika powder, hot
- 1 prize   Ground cinnamon
- 0.5 TL   salt
- 1 prize   Pepper, black, ground

for the bechamel sauce

- 50 G Flour
- 50 G Vegetable margarine
- 350 ml   Soy drink
- 1 prize   salt
- 1 prize   Nutmeg, grated
- 1 prize   Pepper, white, ground

PREPARATION

First peel, wash and thinly slice the potatoes. Wash and clean the aubergine and zucchini, cut into thin slices and sprinkle with salt.

Then wash the tomatoes, remove the stem and cut into slices.

Bring the water with a little salt to a boil in a saucepan, add the potato slices and cook over a medium heat for about 8 minutes. Then drain and drain well.

For the tomato sauce, peel off the shallots and garlic and chop finely.

Heat the olive oil in a pan, sauté the garlic and shallots for about 2 minutes until translucent and stir in the tomato paste.

Then deglaze with the vegetable stock, add the canned tomatoes and bring to the boil for 1 minute. Then reduce the heat, season with sugar, thyme, cinnamon, paprika powder, salt and pepper and simmer for about 5 minutes.

Meanwhile, preheat the oven to 180 ° C (fan oven 160 ° C) and grease a baking dish with olive oil.

Now layer half of the aubergine, potato and zucchini slices in the mold and pour the tomato sauce over them. Layer the remaining vegetable slices and cover with the remaining sauce. Finally, put the tomato slices on top.

For the bechamel sauce, melt the margarine in a saucepan, add the flour, stirring constantly, and sweat for about 2 minutes.

Then pour in the soy drink and cook for about 3-4 minutes, stirring, until the sauce is thick and smooth. Finally, season the sauce with salt, pepper and nutmeg.

Now pour the béchamel sauce over the vegan moussaka and bake on the middle rack in the preheated oven for about 45 minutes.

VEGAN LENTIL SOUP

S

Serevings:4

INGREDIENTS

- 250 G Lentils, brown
- 1 Stg leek
- 2 Pc Carrots
- 1 Pc onion
- 2 l Vegetable broth, hot
- 3 Pc Potatoes, waxy
- 1 Tbsp Vegetable oil
- 1 prize salt
- 1 prize Pepper, black, ground
- 1 prize sugar
- 2 Tbsp Parsley, chopped

PREPARATION

First peel the potatoes and carrots, wash them and cut them into small cubes. Peel the onion and finely chop.

Then clean the leek, wash it thoroughly and cut it into fine rings. Put the lentils in a colander, rinse under cold water and drain.

Heat the oil in a stock pot and sauté the lentils, carrots, onions and leeks in it for about 1 minute. Pour in the vegetable stock and bring to the boil.

As soon as the soup boils, reduce the temperature and cover and let the soup simmer gently for about 15 minutes.

Next, add the potato cubes to the soup and simmer for another 15 minutes. Finally, season with salt, pepper and sugar.

Fill the finished vegan lentil soup into soup bowls, sprinkle with the parsley and enjoy.

VEGAN PUMPKIN SOUP

S

Serevings:4

INGREDIENTS

- 1 kg Hokkaido pumpkin
- 300 gl sweet potato
- 500 ml Vegetable broth, hot
- 1 Can Coconut milk, unsweetened, á 400 ml
- 1 Pc onion
- 2 Pc Garlic cloves
- 1 Tbsp Coconut oil
- 15 G Ginger, fresh
- 1 TL Paprika powder, noble sweet
- 0.5 TL turmeric
- 0.5 TL Coriander, ground
- 1 prize Pepper, black, freshly ground

- 1 prize   salt
- 2 Tbsp   Olive oil, for brushing
- 2 Tbsp   Parsley, chopped

PREPARATION

First preheat the oven to 200 ° C top / bottom heat and line a baking sheet with baking paper.

Then wash the sweet potato and prick it several times with a fork. Wash the pumpkin, cut in half and scrape out the seeds including the fibers. Cut the pumpkin into wedges.

Place the potato and pumpkin wedges on the baking sheet and brush with olive oil. Roast in the preheated oven on the middle rack for about 40-45 minutes. Then take it out of the oven, let it cool down for 10 minutes, peel and dice the sweet potatoes.

Peel and finely chop the onion and garlic. Peel the ginger and also finely chop it. Heat the oil in a stock pot over medium heat and sweat the onion and garlic cubes in it for about 2 minutes.

Now add the ginger and fry for 1 minute. Add the potatoes, pumpkin, paprika powder, turmeric and coriander, pour in the coconut milk and the broth and bring everything to a boil. Bring the contents of the pot to the boil for 1 minute, reduce the temperature and simmer gently for another 10 minutes.

Purée finely with the help of a cutting stick. If the soup is still too thick, stir in a little broth. Season to taste with salt and pepper.

The vegan pumpkin soup into preheated soup bowls fill, sprinkle with parsley and enjoy.

VEGAN GUACAMOLE

s

Serevings:4

INGREDIENTS

- 2   Pc Avocados
- 2   Pc Lime, the juice
- 3   Pc clove of garlic
- 1   TL Chili powder, mild
- 1 prize   salt
- 1 prize   Pepper from the grinder

PREPARATION

Halve the avocados, remove the stone and puree the pulp with the lime juice, squeezed garlic and chili powder using a blender.

Season to taste with salt and pepper before serving.

VEGAN BROCCOLI CREAM SOUP WITH WHITE BEANS

Serevings:4

INGREDIENTS

- 1 kpf broccoli
- 400 G   white beans, pre-cooked
- 1 Stg leek
- 2 Pc Garlic cloves
- 800 ml   Vegetable broth
- 1 TL salt
- 0.5 TL   Pepper, freshly ground
- 0.5 TL   Paprika powder

PREPARATION

First clean the leek, wash it well and cut it into fine rings. Peel and dice the garlic. Clean the broccoli, cut into florets and wash.

Then fry the leek and garlic with a dash of vegetable stock in a large saucepan on a medium heat until translucent.

Then add the broccoli florets and cook for about 5 minutes.

Then add the white beans and vegetable stock, bring to the boil, season with salt, pepper and paprika and simmer for about 10 minutes until the broccoli is cooked through.

Finally, mix the soup with a hand blender until creamy and add a little more seasoning if necessary

VANILLA SAUCE WITHOUT SUGAR

Servings:4

INGREDIENTS

- 500 ml milk
- 1.5 Tbsp food starch
- 1 Pc egg yolk
- 1 Pc Vanilla pod
- 3 Tr Stevia, liquid sweetener to taste

PREPARATION

First put the cornstarch in a bowl. Then add the egg yolk to the cornstarch and beat with the whisk of a hand mixer for about 2 minutes.

Then add about 6-7 tablespoons of the milk and beat for another 3-4 minutes.

Next, slit open the vanilla pod, scrape out the pulp and add to the egg milk. Mix with the whisk for another 1 minute.

Now heat the rest of the milk in a saucepan, bring to the boil for 1 minute and then remove from the stove. Stir the vanilla starch milk into the hot milk, stir in thoroughly and place back on the stove.

The vanilla sauce without sugar can, stirring once again boil 1 minute and make sure that they do not burn. Finally - depending on your taste - stir in 2-3 drops of liquid sweetness and let the sauce cool down.

BAKED FENNEL WITH MOZZARELLA

Serevings:4

INGREDIENTS

- 4   Kn fennel
- 2   Pc tomatoes
- 4 Tbsp   Lemon juice
- 250 G Mozzarella
- 1 Pc   Bay leaf
- 1   between   rosemary
- 1   between   thyme
- 150 ml   White wine, dry
- 350 ml   Vegetable broth
- 1 prize   salt
- 1 prize   Ground pepper
- 2 Tbsp   Oil, for greasing

PREPARATION

First preheat the oven to 200 ° C top and bottom heat / 180 ° C convection and grease a casserole dish with a little oil.

Then wash and dry the fennel, cut off the hard ends and cut into fine strips.

Now put the wine together with the vegetable stock in a saucepan, bring everything to a boil and simmer over medium heat for 4-6 minutes.

In the meantime, wash, dry and finely chop the rosemary and thyme.

Then add the chopped herbs together with the bay leaf and a pinch of salt and pepper to the pot.

Then add the fennel to the pot and cook it for 4-6 minutes.

Meanwhile, drain the mozzarella and cut into slices.

Then wash the tomatoes, dry them and also cut them into thin slices.

In the next step, drain the fennel, drain well, place in the baking dish and drizzle with the lemon juice.

Finally, put the tomatoes and mozzarella in the baking dish and bake the fennel in the oven for around 10 minutes.

FANTASTICALLY SWEET YEAST DOUGH

Serevings:1

- **INGREDIENTS**
- 500 G Spelled flour type 630
- 250 ml   Soy drink
- 120 G Raw cane sugar
- 1 prize   salt
- 2 Tbsp   Sunflower oil
- 42 G Fresh yeast

PREPARATION

First crumble the yeast cube in a dough bowl, add the soy drink and 2 tablespoons of raw cane sugar, stir briefly and let rest for about 10 minutes.

Then add the flour, salt, sunflower oil and the remaining raw cane sugar and knead everything thoroughly for several minutes, ideally with a food processor or a slow hand mixer with a dough hook.

As soon as a smooth, even batter has formed, moisten a clean tea towel and place it over the bowl. Finally, put it in a warm place for about four hours so that the dough can rise in peace.

Depending on the additional recipe for which the wonderfully sweet yeast dough is used, the baking time is around 30 minutes at 180 ° C (convection).

TOMATOSOUP

S

Serevings:4

INGREDIENTS

- 1 l   light bone broth
- 500 G tomatoes
- 60 G   butter
- 50 G   Root system
- 1 Pc   onion
- 40 G   Flour
- 1 shot vinegar
- 1 TL   sugar
- 0.5 TL   Peppercorns
- 1 TL   salt
- 2 Pc   garlic

PREPARATION

Peel or clean the roots, peel the onion and garlic and cut the ingredients into small pieces. Roast some peppercorns with a little butter.

Lightly sweat the whole thing with a little flour and pour 1 liter of bone soup on top.

Then tear up the skinned tomatoes and stir into the broth with tomato paste.

The soup is cooked for another 25 minutes with salt, vinegar and sugar.

Finally, finely strain the tomato soup using a sieve.

TOMATO SOUP WITHOUT SUGAR

Serevings:2

INGREDIENTS

- 100   GMicrowave popcorn, lightly salted
- 3   Pc   Carrots
- 10 Pc Cocktail tomatoes, red
- 0.5   l Vegetable broth
- 0.5 Pc onion
- 1 prize   salt
- 1 prize   Pepper, black, ground

PREPARATION

First let the popcorn puff up in the microwave for about 3-4 minutes, then remove it and set it aside.

Peel, wash and grate the carrots on a sharp grater. Bring the vegetable stock to a boil in a saucepan, add the carrots and cook for about 12-15 minutes until soft.

Meanwhile, wash the tomatoes and cut them in half. Peel the onions and cut into fine wedges. Add tomatoes and onions to the soup and simmer for another 30 minutes over low heat.

Finally puree everything finely with a cutting stick and bring to the boil for another 1 minute.

The tomato soup without sugar to taste with salt and pepper and place in a warm plate. Add the popcorn to the soup as a topping and serve.

TOMATO SOUP WITH RICE

S

Serevings:4

INGREDIENTS

- 2   Pc   onion
- 2   Tbsp   Olive oil, for the pot
- 150 G Long grain rice
- 1   l   Tomato juice
- 1   TL   salt
- 1 prize   Pepper White
- 0.5 TL   sugar
- 3 TbspParsley, freshly chopped
- 0.5 TL   Marjoram, finely chopped

PREPARATION

For the tomato soup with rice, first peel and finely chop the onions. Then heat the oil in a saucepan and sauté the onion pieces in it.

Then wash the rice, add to the onions and stir-fry for 1-2 minutes.

Then pour in the tomato juice, sprinkle in the marjoram, salt and pepper, bring to the boil and simmer covered over low heat for about 15-20 minutes until the rice is cooked.

Finally, season the soup again with salt, pepper and sugar, sprinkle with chopped parsley and serve garnished with a basil leaf.

TOMATO SOUP WITH PEARL BARLEY

Serevings:2

INGREDIENTS

- 1   Can Tomatoes, á 800 g
- 1   Federation Soup greens (celery, carrots, leek)
- 1   Pc   onion
- 1   Pc   clove of garlic
- 75 G   Pearl barley
- 6   Pc Sage leaves
- 1   Tbsp   olive oil
- 750 ml   Vegetable broth
- 6   Tbsp   Creme fraiche Cheese
- 4   Tbsp   Parmesan, freshly grated

- 1 prize   salt
- 1 prize   Pepper, black, freshly ground

PREPARATION

First peel the carrots and celery, then wash and dice. Clean the leek, wash it thoroughly and also cut it into small cubes.

Peel the onion and garlic and dice very finely. Then wash the sage and cut it into fine strips.

Next, heat the olive oil in a soup pot and fry the diced vegetables, onion and garlic in it for about 3-4 minutes. Then add the sage leaves and the pearl barley and fry for 2-3 minutes.

Now add the stock and the juice of the canned tomatoes. Roughly chop the canned tomatoes and add them as well.

The tomato soup with pearl barley can then simmer for about 30 minutes at medium temperature.

Finally stir in the crème fraîche and the grated Parmesan cheese into the soup, season with salt and pepper and serve hot.

TOMATO RAGOUT WITH EGGPLANT

Serevings:4

INGREDIENTS

- 2 Pc Eggplant, medium size
- 4 Pc Tomatoes, great
- 2 Pc Garlic cloves
- 2 Tbsp   Basil, chopped
- 1 prize   salt
- 1 TL olive oil
- 1 prize   pepper

PREPARATION

Peel the garlic cloves, press them through a garlic press and sauté lightly in a pan with oil.

Remove the stalk from the eggplant, peel, cut into small cubes and mix in the pan with the garlic.

Then wash the tomatoes, cut them into small pieces and also mix in the pan. Fry the vegetables in the pan for about 6-8 minutes - stirring constantly.

Then season with salt, pepper and fresh basil to taste and serve with white bread.

TOMATOES FILLED WITH SPINACH

Serevings: 4

INGREDIENTS

- 4 Pc Beefsteak tomatoes
- 1 Pc onion
- 2 Pc Garlic cloves
- 175 G Spinach leaves
- 2 Tbsp olive oil
- 60 G Sheep cheese
- 3 Tbsp Gratin cheese (grated)
- 1 prize salt and pepper
- 1 prize Nutmeg (ground)

PREPARATION

Cut off a lid from the washed tomatoes, scrape out the pulp with a spoon and place the tomatoes in an oiled baking dish.

Wash and drain the spinach.

Peel onion and garlic, chop finely and sauté in hot olive oil until translucent. Then add the spinach, stew until al dente and mix with the sheep's cheese.

Then season the spinach mixture with nutmeg, salt and pepper, pour into the tomatoes, sprinkle the grated cheese on top and place the tomatoes filled with spinach in the preheated oven (180 ° C) for 10 minutes.

TOMATOES WRAPPED IN CUCUMBER

Serevings:2

INGREDIENTS

- 8 Pc Cocktail tomatoes
- 1 shot olive oil
- 2 Pc Cucumbers
- 1 prize Spices (salt, pepper, etc.)

PREPARATION

Remove the ends of the cucumber and cut lengthways into thin slices. Place the cucumber slices on the work surface. Put one tomato on each and wrap it tightly.

So that the whole thing holds together, it is fixed with toothpicks. Just season, brush with olive oil and place on the hot grill (5-7 min.)

COLD TOMATO BOWL

S

Serevings:4

INGREDIENTS

- 1   kg Tomatoes, canned, diced
- 4   Pc clove of garlic
- 3   between   basil
- 600 ml   Vegetable broth
- 1 Pc Orange, juice
- 1 prize   salt

PREPARATION

At the beginning peel and finely chop the garlic, also finely chop the washed basil.

Now bring the tomatoes, garlic, orange juice, basil and broth to the boil in a large saucepan and simmer for a few minutes over low heat.

Then puree the soup with the blender, add salt to taste and cover and chill for at least 4 hours.

TOMATO AND CUCUMBER STICKS

Serevings:2

INGREDIENTS

- 8   Pc Cherry tomatoes
- 1 prize   salt
- 1 Pc   Cucumber
- 1 prize   Pepper (freshly ground)
- 1 shot olive oil
- 8   Pc   Toothpick (to fix)

PREPARATION

Wash the cucumber and cut lengthways into wafer-thin slices with a peeler.

Then place the cucumber slices on the worktop and season with salt and pepper. Now place the washed tomatoes on one of the ends, roll up tightly and fix with a toothpick.

Then brush with olive oil, place on the hot grill (or oven / grill) and grill for about 5 minutes.

THAI SWEET AND SOUR SAUCE

S

Serevings:4

INGREDIENTS

- 1   Pc   red peppers, great
- 2   Pc   Garlic cloves
- 1   Pc   Chilli pepper
- 5   Tbsp   Rice vinegar
- 10Tbsp   sugar
- 250 ml   water

PREPARATION

In the first step, wash the peppers, cut in half, core and cut into small pieces, do the same with the chilli pepper.

Then peel the garlic, chop it roughly and put it in the blender along with the pieces of pepper, chilli pieces, vinegar and water.

Then puree the whole thing for about a minute and then pour it into a small saucepan.

Now add sugar, stir in and simmer on low heat while stirring until the sauce thickens.

Then let it cool down and serve the finished Thai sweet and sour sauce in a bowl or over a dish.

SWEET POTATOES WITH COTTAGE CHEESE

Serevings: 3

INGREDIENTS

- 2   Pc Sweet potatoes
- 2   Pc   Carrots
- 3 Tbsp   Basil leaves
- 200 G Cottage cheese, cream cheese
- 1 prize   salt
- 1 prize   Paprika powder, noble sweet
- 1 prize   Ground pepper
- 3 Tbsp   Parsley, fresh

PREPARATION

First preheat the oven to 200 ° C top and bottom heat / 180 ° C circulating air.

In the meantime, wash and peel the sweet potatoes, cut into 6 equal slices or pieces, place on a baking sheet and bake in the oven for about 10 minutes.

In the meantime, wash and peel the carrots and grate them finely in a bowl with a kitchen grater.

Then wash the basil, shake it dry and finely chop it with a knife.

Then add the cottage cheese to the bowl and mix with salt, pepper, paprika and basil.

Now wash, dry and finely chop the parsley.

Finally, remove the sweet potatoes from the oven, brush with the cottage cheese and garnish with the parsley.

SWEET POTATO SALAD WITH SPINACH

Serevings:4

INGREDIENTS

- 4 Pc   Medium sized sweet potatoes
- 150   G   Spinach, young
- 16   Pc Cherry tomatoes
- 80   G Pine nuts
- 4 Tbsp   olive oil
- 1 prize   salt
- 1 prize pepper
- 1 Pc   avocado

for the dressing

- 3 Tbsp   Honey, liquid
- 3 Tbsp   Red wine vinegar

- 2 Tbsp   olive oil
- 1 prize   salt
- 1 prize   pepper

PREPARATION

First peel and wash the sweet potatoes and cut them into even, thin wedges.

Sort the spinach, wash it thoroughly and dry it. Wash the cherry tomatoes and cut in half.

Now roast the pine nuts in a coated pan without fat - stir constantly, then take them out of the pan and let them cool down.

Now heat 4 tablespoons of olive oil in a non-stick pan, fry the sweet potato wedges in it over a moderate heat for about 15 minutes and season with salt and pepper.

Then peel the avocado, remove the stone and cut into thin wedges.

Now put the honey, vinegar and olive oil in a bowl, whisk thoroughly with the blender and season with salt and pepper.

Finally, distribute the spinach and avocado in the middle of the plates, then decorate the sweet potatoes with the tomatoes, drizzle with the dressing and serve the sweet potato salad with spinach sprinkled with the pine nuts.

SWEET POTATO CURRY CHIPS

S

Serevings:2

INGREDIENTS

- 2   Pc Sweet potato, great
- 2 Tbsp   Oil, neutral
- 1 TL   curry
- 1 TL   salt
- 1 prize   Pepper, freshly ground

PREPARATION

Preheat the oven to 180 degrees and cover a baking sheet with baking paper.

Then wash the sweet potato thoroughly, cut it into thin slices or slice it and place it on the baking sheet.

Drizzle with oil and season with salt, pepper and curry, then bake the sweet potato curry chips in the hot oven for 20 minutes.

SWEET CARROTS

S

Serevings:4

INGREDIENTS

- 700 G Carrots, small
- 1 Tbsp   butter
- 3 Tbsp honey

PREPARATION

Wash and clean the carrots beforehand and cover with a little water and let them simmer over low heat.

Then heat the butter in a pan over medium heat, add the honey and the carrots and glaze the carrots while stirring constantly on a low heat. This takes about 1 to 2 minutes.

SWEET PUMPKIN RAW FOOD

S

Serevings:3

INGREDIENTS

- 1   Pc   Hokkaido pumpkin, small
- 1 prize   Vanilla, ground
- 1 prize   Organic cinnamon, Ceylon variety
- 2 Tbsp   Maple syrup (more if necessary)

PREPARATION

First, wash the pumpkin, cut it in half, remove the stone and grate it with a kitchen grater.

Then put the pulp in a nice bowl, stir in the vanilla, maple syrup and cinnamon and enjoy the finished, sweet raw pumpkin .

SWEET AND SOUR CHINESE CABBAGE SALAD

Serevings:2

INGREDIENTS

- 1   Pc   Chinese cabbage

for the dressing

- 2 Tbsp   soy sauce
- 1 TL   honey
- 1 Tbsp   Rice vinegar
- 2 Pc   clove of garlic

PREPARATION

Remove the stalk from the Chinese cabbage, wash the leaves well and cut into strips. Then peel and finely chop the garlic.

Then stir in a dressing with the garlic, soy sauce, rice vinegar and honey.

Marinate the sweet and sour Chinese cabbage salad with it and chill for 15 minutes before serving.

TURBOT WITH SEAWEED AND ORANGE SALAD

Serevings:4

INGREDIENTS

- 1.5 carton Turbot
- 50 G Seaweed, dried, e.g. wakame, sea spaghetti
- 2 Pc Oranges
- 2 Tbsp sesame oil
- 2 TL Wine vinegar
- 2 TL Honey, liquid
- 2 Msp salt
- 20 ml Rapeseed oil
- 1 TL sea-salt
- 0.5 TL Pepper, dark, freshly ground

PREPARATION

Fillet the whole turbot. Leave the skin on the two fillets on the light side and remove the skin on the two fillets on the dark and grainy side.

Then soak the algae in cold water for 30 minutes, place in a sieve, rinse well with cold water and bring to the boil in a saucepan with plenty of water. Simmer gently for 20 minutes, then drain and let cool. Roughly cut the seaweed and place in a bowl.

Now remove the peel from the oranges with a sharp knife, remove the fillets and set aside. Squeeze the juice out of the orange meat and add to the algae. Also add sesame oil, vinegar and honey to the algae and mix well. Before serving, mix in the orange fillets and season with the 2 pinches of salt.

Cut the turbot fillets into portions. Put the rapeseed oil in a coated pan and place the fillets (those with the skin on the skin side) inside. Do not season the fillets beforehand. Now heat the pan slowly but steadily and let the fillets lie on their side until they are nice and brown and crispy (3–4 minutes).

Then turn the fillets over and reduce the temperature of the pan. Continue to cook the fillets at the remaining temperature of the pan until they are done and still have a juicy core. Season the fillets with sea salt and pepper before serving.

To serve, arrange some of the algae-orange salad in the middle of the plate and add a freshly roasted piece of fillet.

MUSTARD CRUST STEAK

S

Serevings:4

INGREDIENTS

- 2 Tbsp   breadcrumbs
- 1 Pc egg
- 1 Tbsp   Nuts, ground
- 4 Pc Beef steaks (approx. 200 grams each)
- 8 Pc Peppercorns
- 0.5 TL   salt
- 4 Tbsp   mustard
- 4 Tbspoil

PREPARATION

Wash steaks in cold water and pat dry. Rub with freshly ground pepper. Preheat the oven to 200 degrees.

Sear the steaks in clarified butter. Let sit for 2 minutes on each side (turn only once).

Beat the egg with salt and pepper over a hot water bath until frothy. Mix in the breadcrumbs, nuts and mustard. Place the steaks in a greased casserole dish, spread the mustard mixture on the steaks, place in the oven and bake for 5 minutes.

POINTED PEPPERS FILLED WITH TOFU

Serevings:4

INGREDIENTS

- 8   Pc   Pointed peppers
- 200 ml   Vegetable broth, for the baking dish
- 1   shot Olive oil to drizzle with

for the filling

- 4   Pc   spring onions
- 2   Pc   clove of garlic
- 10 Pc Cherry tomatoes
- 1   Tbsp   Olive oil, for the pan
- 160 G tofu
- 200 G Chickpeas, canned
- 1   TL   Curry powder

- 0.5 TL   Ground cumin
- 3 Tbsp   Lemon juice
- 1 Tbsp   Mint leaves, cut into strips
- 1 TL   salt
- 0.5 TL   Cayenne pepper
- 120 G Natural yoghurt

PREPARATION

Cut a lid off the top of the peppers and remove the seeds without damaging the skin.

Then clean and finely chop the spring onions. Cut the cherry tomatoes into very small pieces.

Now peel the garlic, chop it finely and sweat it together with the spring onions in a pan in hot oil for 2 minutes. Then add the tomato pieces and fry them briefly.

Cut the tofu into small pieces and add to the pan with the chickpeas, bring to the boil briefly and season with curry, caraway seeds, lemon juice, mint, salt and cayenne pepper.

Then stir in the yoghurt and pour the mixture into the peppers (with a piping nozzle) - put the pepper lid back on.

Finally, pour the vegetable stock into a baking dish, put in the filled peppers, drizzle a little olive oil and cook in a preheated oven at 180 degrees (top-bottom heat) for around 30 minutes.

POINTED PEPPERS WITH COUSCOUS

Serevings:4

INGREDIENTS

- 3 Pc   leek
- 120 G couscous
- 180 ml   Vegetable broth
- 1 Pc   lemon
- 0.5 Can   Chickpeas, about 150g
- 2 Tbsp   olive oil
- 120 G Cherry tomatoes
- 180 G Mushrooms, small
- 4   Pc Pointed peppers
- 20   G Parmesan, freshly grated

for the tomato sauce

- 1 prize   salt
- 1 prize   pepper
- 2 Pc   clove of garlic
- 1 Can Tomato pieces, about 400g
- 2 TL   Oregano, dried
- 1 TL   sugar
- 2 Tbsp   Olive oil, for the pot
- 1 prize   Chilli powder

PREPARATION

First, preheat the oven to 200 ° C fan oven.

Then bring the vegetable stock to the boil in a saucepan, remove from the heat, add the couscous and let it soak for about 10 minutes - until the couscous has absorbed the stock.

In the meantime, clean and wash the leek and cut into rings. Wash the lemon with hot water, rub dry, grate the peel finely and squeeze the juice out of the lemon.

Drain the chickpeas through a sieve, rinse with cold water and drain well.

Now add half of the spring onions, chickpeas, lemon juice, lemon zest and olive oil to the couscous and mix - season with salt and pepper.

For the tomato sauce, peel the garlic, cut it into fine slices, heat it with a little oil in a small saucepan and roast it until golden brown.

Then add the tomato pieces (including juice) from the can, bring to the boil and season with oregano, chili powder, sugar and salt and pepper.

Now wash the cherry tomatoes and cut them in half. Clean and clean the mushrooms and also cut them in half. Wash the pointed peppers, pat dry, halve each lengthwise and remove the seeds.

Then put the tomato sauce in an ovenproof baking dish, spread the halved cherry tomatoes and mushrooms in it.

Fill the pepper halves with the couscous mixture and also place in the baking dish - with the filling facing up.

Finally, grate the parmesan cheese finely and sprinkle the stuffed peppers with it. Put the baking dish in the oven and bake for about 30 minutes.

POINTED CABBAGE WITH DRESSING

Serevings:4

INGREDIENTS

- 1200 G cabbage
- 2000ml Vegetable broth
- 2 Federation radish
- 2 Tbsp Capers
- 0.5 Federation parsley
- 1 Pc Medium onion
- 350 G Whole milk yogurt, creamy
- 4 Tbsp milk
- 2 prize salt
- 2 prize pepper
- 1 prize sugar

PREPARATION

First remove the outer, wilted leaves from the pointed cabbage, then wash and quarter the pointed cabbage, remove the stalk and cut into strips.

Then the vegetable broth to boil in a pot and pieces of coal is in 4 portions for about 5 minutes blanch . Then remove with a slotted spoon, place in a sieve, rinse with cold water, cool and drain.

Now clean, wash and cut the radishes into small cubes. Halve the capers. Wash the parsley, shake dry, pluck the leaves from the stems and cut into strips. Peel the onion and cut into fine cubes.

Now mix the yoghurt and milk well in a bowl, stir in the radishes, capers, parsley and onions and season well with salt, pepper and sugar.

Finally, place the pointed cabbage on 4 plates, arrange the dressing in the middle and serve sprinkled with a little pepper.

ASPARAGUS WITH SALMON FILLET FROM THE STEAMER

Serevings:4

INGREDIENTS

- 500 G salmon
- 500 G Asparagus, white
- 1 prize pepper
- 1 prize salt
- 1 prize sugar
- 1 Tbsp Lemon juice
- 1 prize Cress, finely chopped, for garnish
- 1 Pc Spring onion

PREPARATION

First wash the white asparagus, cut off the lower woody ends, peel the asparagus and place in a perforated steamer - sprinkle with a little sugar, salt and pepper. If possible, you should choose asparagus stalks of roughly the same thickness so that they cook evenly.

Then wash the salmon fillet, pat dry, drizzle with a little lemon juice and sprinkle with salt and pepper.

Put the salmon and the finely chopped spring onions in another perforated steamer.

Now place the two steamer containers in the steamer and cook at around 90 degrees for around 15 minutes.

If the asparagus stalks are not soft after the cooking time, remove the fish and let the asparagus cook for a few more minutes.

ASPARAGUS FROM THE ROMAN POT

Serevings:2

INGREDIENTS

- 500 G Asparagus, white
- 1 prize salt
- 1 prize sugar
- 3 Tbsp Lemon juice
- 2 Tbsp water

PREPARATION

At the beginning, water the Römertopf, ie put it in water for at least 10 minutes, this will fill the clay pores and steam will be produced during cooking.

Wash the asparagus, cut off the hard ends and peel. Season with salt, sugar and lemon juice and place in the Römertopf.

Then pour in the water and place covered in the cold oven. Now heat up to 190 degrees circulating air and cook the asparagus in the Roman pot for 60 minutes.

Tips on the recipe

If the asparagus spears are very thick, the cooking time may be a little longer.

ASPARAGUS FROM THE STEAMER WITH WILD GARLIC PESTO

Serevings:4

INGREDIENTS

- 1 kg Asparagus, white
- 1 TL sugar

for the wild garlic pesto

- 30 G Pine nuts
- 80 G Wild garlic leaves
- 1 Federation Parsley, roughly chopped
- 30 G Parmesan cheese, grated
- 100 ml Extra virgin olive oil
- 1 TL Lemon juice
- 1 prize salt

- 1 prize   pepper
- 1 Pc   Clove of garlic, peeled

PREPARATION

Peel the asparagus with an asparagus knife and cut off the woody ends (approx. 2-3 cm).

Boil the asparagus peels and the end pieces in a saucepan with water for 5 minutes.

Then layer the asparagus in the perforated steamer insert, add a little sugar and steam for about 10 minutes at 100 ° C. To do this, the steamer is filled with the asparagus water.

For the wild garlic pesto, first roast the pine nuts in a non-stick pan (without fat).

Then mix or puree the washed and chopped wild garlic, peeled garlic clove and parsley with the parmesan, pine nuts and oil.

Finally add a little lemon juice, salt and pepper and spread the pesto over the warm asparagus.

SIMPLE RAW SALAD DRESSING

S

Serevings:1

INGREDIENTS

- 100 ml water
- 3 Tbsp Sunflower seeds
- 0.5 Pc lemon
- 1 Pc clove of garlic
- 2 Tbsp 6 herb mixture
- 1 prize salt and pepper

PREPARATION

First, squeeze the lemon half, peel the garlic and chop it roughly.

Then put lemon juice, garlic, water, sunflower seeds, herbs and salt and pepper in a small blender and puree for 30 seconds.

SELLERY SOUP

S

Servings:4

INGREDIENTS

- Pc onion
- 500 G   celery root
- 25 G butter
- 700 ml   Vegetable broth
- 200 ml   Milk, low fat
- 1 prize   salt
- 1 prize pepper
- 1 Msp nutmeg

PREPARATION

Wash, peel and cut the celery into large pieces. Peel the onions, chop them finely and sauté them in a saucepan with butter.

Then add the broth, celery, salt, pepper and nutmeg and cook covered for about 20 minutes at a lower temperature.

Then add the milk and puree the soup with the hand blender. Season again to taste and just warm up more.

CONCLUSION

If you want to lose a few pounds, the low-carb and low-fat diet will eventually reach your limits. Although the weight can be reduced with the diets, the success is usually only short-lived because the diets are too one-sided. So if you want to lose weight and avoid a classic yo-yo effect, you should rather check your energy balance and recalculate your daily calorie requirement.

The ideal is to adhere to a gentle variant of the low-fat diet with 60 to 80 grams of fat per day for life. It helps to maintain the weight and protects against diabetes and high blood lipids with all their health risks.

The low-fat diet is comparably easy to implement because you only have to forego fatty foods or severely limit their proportion of the daily amount of food. With the low-carb diet, on the other hand, much more precise planning and more stamina are necessary. Anything that really fills you up is usually high in carbohydrates and should be avoided. Under certain circumstances, this can lead to food cravings and thus to failure of the diet. It is essential that you eat properly. Many statutory health insurance companies therefore offer prevention courses or pay you for individual nutritional advice. Such advice is extremely important, especially if you decide on a weight-loss diet in which you want to permanently change your entire diet. Whether your private health insurance pays for such measures depends on the tariff you have taken out. In the meantime, however, individual nutritional advice has been taken over by many private providers.